Clay Perry's

fantastic
flowers

Clay Perry's
fantastic
flowers

with text by Maggie Perry

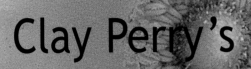

contents

PAGES 2–3 *Ranunculus* 'Rembrandt'
PAGES 5–6 *Gerbera* 'Transvaal Daisy'
Parade series cultivar
OPPOSITE: The wonderful furled trumpets of the Calla
Lily, *Zantedeschia* 'mango'.

introduction

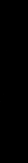

Over the years I have had the privilege of working in some of the world's most beautiful gardens for various books and publications. Hidcote Manor, Sissinghurst, Rousham, Hestercombe, West Green, Wollerton Old Hall and many others, both in the UK and abroad, have all entranced me. Yet when I started working in these gardens, I was interested more in their atmosphere and landscape architecture than in their detail. My main aim was to capture the structure and unique quality of each place, to create a timelessness in an ever-changing environment. The search for the perfect viewpoint and the constantly changing light were my main preoccupations. It is only comparatively recently that I have become more absorbed by detail, most particularly in the shapes and forms of flowers.

It was my wife Maggie who first taught me to look closely at flowers. We were living in Norfolk, and in the spring and early summer the lanes and woods were full of wildflowers. Maggie knew the names of just about all of them and I became fascinated by their succession through spring into summer. From the first little golden stars of aconites and celandines under clouds of blackthorn blossom, the delicate primroses – flowers of decadence – and the serried ranks of Jack-by-the-hedge among fresh hawthorn leaves, to the filigree delicacy of Queen Anne's lace and the voluptuous pungency of May blossom, they were all unique. It is strange to reflect that this interest kindled in the country lanes of Norfolk has led us, years later, on obsessive journeys through the Australian desert, into tropical rainforests and up Cretan mountainsides in search of rare and perfect blooms.

Although I had been photographing flowers in their natural environment for a while, it was working on *David Austin's English Roses* in studio conditions that gave me the opportunity to observe flowers in a completely different way. I found time to reflect on the subtleties of the play of light on petals, buds and leaves, and began to see the flowers in the way that perhaps the Dutch masters had seen them, in an altered state that seemed somehow symbolic. It was my interest in this emblematic state that led to my book *Medieval Flowers*, in which I was able to take this further, while at the same time leading me back to my early Norfolk days.

In this book I have tried to emphasise what is so fantastic about flowers of all kinds. There is an extraordinary diversity among them, from a lily-of-the-valley, with its delicate perfumed bells to the scaly talons of a heliconia or the amazing architectural structure of a euphorbia. Then there is the blatantly erotic form of a dragona (which exudes the smell of rotten meat to attract the flies that pollinate it), the sensual translucency of an iris, or the gross indecency of a banana flower. Yet the fantastic can also be found in more familiar flowers, in the simple forms of a geranium with its delicate veined petals, or the impudent painted face of a pansy.

Working on this book has been a fascinating journey for me and an opportunity to collaborate with Maggie. I would like to thank Kyle Cathie for making this possible, and to express my hope that the book may bring as much pleasure to others as it has to us.

LEFT: The beautifully translucent flowers of *Hippeastrum* 'Christmas Gift'.
OVELEAF: *Iris* 'Olympic Challenger'.

a-z of flowers

Acanthus (Acanthaceae)

acanthus

The seemingly lifeless sun-baked olive groves of Greece hold infinite delights if you know where to look. Acanthus, with its wonderful scrolled foliage and stems of softly hued flowers, is one of the treasures to be found there. It is a glorious adjunct to any border, bringing a hint of Ancient Greece to the modern world.

Named from *akanthos*, the Greek for thorn, the plant is native to the arid stony terrain of the Mediterranean. Acanthus is one of the most impressive architectural garden plants, with handsome jagged foliage and stiff spikes of claw-shaped flowers that range in colour from white, green and pink through to purple. It is particularly useful as a mid-border filler, producing its statuesque flower spikes from early summer until the first frosts.

As a genus Acanthus consists of some 30 species. Of those in cultivation *A. spinosus* is the most common, chosen for its neat habit and purple-and-white hooded flowers. It has been cultivated as a decorative plant since the classical era, and was a particular inspiration for the Greek sculptor Callimachos in the fifth century BC. It is said that on seeing the plant growing on a girl's grave in Corinth he was moved to carve its leaves on stone columns. Eventually Corinthian architecture became defined by the presence of carved acanthus leaves. The leaves were subsequentally adopted by the Romans as a decoration on buildings, fabrics and ceramics, and they are still popular as a design today.

Pliny, the Roman scholar writing in the first century AD, mentions acanthus growing in his garden, but unlike many other plants, he says relatively little about its herbal uses. Dioscorides, a Greek physician of the same era, describes the roots as being beneficial for cramp and consumption.

Acanthus was listed as a garden plant in the twelfth century by Alexander Neckham, an English scholar and foster brother to Richard Coeur de Lyon. He described it in his *De naturis rerum* (*On the nature of things*), which was the main reference compendium of plants grown in monastery gardens.

Acanthus were cultivated in physick gardens until the seventeenth century. The plants' burn-relieving properties were noted by Parkinson in 1629 in his *Paradisus in sole paradisus terrestris* which can be seen as a pun on his name, park-in-sun's earthly paradise. He recommended crushing the leaves and soaking them in cold water before applying.

In the nineteenth century, they enjoyed a revival in popularity because of their handsome foliage, which could be used to create the ornate gardens fashionable at this time.

Today, these hardy aristocrats are justifiably in demand with gardeners worldwide, for they add form and stature to any border, and are spectacular when grown in containers. The cut stems are excellent for indoor flower arrangements; they also retain their gentle colours after drying. But beware when cutting them – under their flowers most species have sharp spines lurking that are easily shed and very painful.

TOP RIGHT: *A. spinosus* makes an interesting contrast to feverfew in a garden border.
LEFT: *Acanthus spinosus*, shown here growing with the feathery plumes of astilbe, can reach at least 1.2m (4ft) in height.
OPPOSITE: A densely packed flower stem of *A. spinosus* reveals its treacherous spines.

FLOWERING SEASON: Early to late summer.
SOIL CONDITIONS: Any soil that drains freely.
SITUATE: In open dappled shade or full sunshine.
PROPAGATION: Sow seeds in situ in autumn or in a cold frame in spring, when they should be planted in a suitable loam-based compost. Autumn root cuttings are simple to grow.
RESILIENCE: Mostly hardy.
CARE: Keep watered while growing. Cover with straw in severe winters for extra protection.

FLOWERING SEASON: From the middle of summer to the beginning of autumn.
SOIL CONDITIONS: Free-draining rich soil.
SITUATE: In full sun.
PROPAGATION: Seed should be sown in spring and protected from frost under glass. It is easy to divide existing plants.
RESILIENCE: Hardy to frost-tender.
CARE: Keep pots well watered when flowering and less so when dormant. Beware of slugs and snails.

Agapanthus (Alliaceae), African blue lily

agapanthus

Agapanthus are stunning. I first encountered them in profusion in Madeira, a jewel of an island bedecked with flowers. Even there, the great drumstick-like blooms in deep blue or virginal white were impressive. Their delicacy of form not only looks outstanding from a distance, but bears close scrutiny, too.

The agapanthus was brought to Europe from its native South Africa in the early seventeenth century and was described as *Hyacinthus africanus tuberosus*. Plants were grown in the garden of Hampton Court Palace in England from 1692 and caused a sensation when they first bloomed in 1697. Originally given the name African blue lily, today they are known

more widely by their Latin name, which comes from the Greek words *agape*, meaning to love, and *anthos*, a flower.

Agapanthus are hard to beat as ornamentals in the garden. In summer they produce dramatic loose globes of blue or white lily-like flowers on slender stems above a fountain of lush green foliage. Although they have a reputation for being tender, many half and fully-hardy varieties are now available.

The 'Headbourne Hybrids' are perhaps the hardiest form, but vary in shades of blue because many are raised from seed. Also hardy is 'Cherry Holley', which bears open dark blue flowers in mid-summer, and often flowers again in the early autumn. Of the white-flowered forms, 'Alice Gloucester' is frost-hardy, forming a tall plant, up to 1m (3ft) high, with trumpet-shaped blooms towards the end of summer.

Dwarf forms exist, useful for the front of a border, in containers or even a rockery. *Agapanthus africanus* 'Albus' bears white blooms and reaches 60cm (24in), while the diminutive *A.* 'Tinkerbell' grows to just 45cm (18in) and has silver-striped leaves and pale blue flowers.

In large warmer gardens the less hardy varieties can be planted in vast swathes of either white or blue. They also look extremely impressive in smaller borders and beds. Container-grown they are hard to surpass and look wonderful on steps and patios or placed next to a pond, where their elegant form can be seen to best advantage in the shimmering reflection. They are also ideal candidates for a temperate conservatory, which offers an environment similar to that of their native climate.

If you grow hardy varieties, plants can be left outside during the winter months and the seed-heads left for winter interest. On well-drained soil more tender varieties may survive the winter if protected with bracken or straw.

Large bunches of agapanthus can now be bought from the florist. They are extraordinarily long-lived as a cut flower, and can be enjoyed at home even if you are unable to grow these graceful creatures yourself.

THIS PAGE: The dramatic flowerheads of *Agapanthus campanulatus* subs. *patens*.

Allium (Alliaceae), ornamental onion

allium

Great puffs of alliums standing to attention in the garden are a beguiling sight. Resembling exclamation marks in a border, alliums command attention. They continue to be attractive long after the flowers fade because the seedheads are equally appealing. Planted in well-placed urns or pots – in corners, at the end of walkways – they draw the eye without being too blatant, and are easily controlled.

The culinary alliums (namely leek, onion and garlic) have been grown for so long that their origins are lost in the mists of time. Garlic, *Allium sativum*, was valued for its potent flavour, but also for its great power against magical spells and vampires. In Homer's *Odyssey* Hermes advises Odysseus to eat garlic to protect him from Circe the sorceress, while the Greek physician Dioscorides recommended it as a tonic, as a drug for expelling worms from the digestive system, and to combat asthma. Even today the children of Gascony in France are baptised with a clove of garlic on the lips to promote health and vitality, and also perhaps to avert the evil eye. Garlic also has a worldwide reputation as a natural antiseptic and cleanser of the blood.

The wood garlic or ramsons, *A. ursinum*, is the native wild garlic of woodlands throughout the northern hemisphere and has long been used in cooking. John Gerard, the sixteenth-century herbalist, wrote that the leaves 'maye very well

LEFT AND OPPOSITE: Two examples of the varied allium species – the delicate flowers of *A. bulgaricum* (left) and the dramatic spikes of *A. cristophii* (opposite).

be eaten in April and Maie with butter, as such are of a strong constitution, and labouring men'. We may no longer care to eat wood garlic but, in a garden setting, combined with bluebells, pheasant's eye (*Narcissus majalis*) and Queen Anne's lace or cow parsley (the gentle umbellifer *Anthriscus sylvestris*) it can help create a 'flowery mead', a medieval style of wildflower planting.

Chives (*A. schoenoprasum*) were grown decoratively by the Elizabethans and are long-standing inhabitants of the kitchen garden, where they make a wonderful edging for ornamental potagers and vegetable plots. At that time all the alliums were referred to as 'molies', the name that Homer used. This name is retained by the golden garlic, *A. moly*, said by Pliny to be the most precious. It grows just 22cm (9in) tall and produces clusters of bright yellow, star-shaped flowers in mid-summer.

The Egyptian tree onion (*A. cepa*) from Central Asia, is a wonderful oddity, bearing no flowers but a cluster of tiny onions at the top of its stem. It has only recently gone out of use in the kitchen garden. Possibly one of the earliest species grown as a crop, this crown of onions was still being sold in Covent Garden market in London in the late nineteenth century.

Ornamental alliums slipped from favour, mostly because of their great propensity to multiply and invade the garden. However, the intrepid plant collectors of the late nineteenth century rekindled interest in them and new species arrived from Asia, *A. cristophii* and *A. giganteum* being two of the most spectacular examples.

The entire genus contains 700 species growing in the northern hemisphere and the highly decorative alliums are now deeply fashionable in all their guises. There is a vast choice readily available; perhaps the best known is *A. giganteum*, which bears huge globes of mauve star-shaped flowers on top of stiff 1.2m (4ft) stems in early summer. More difficult to grow, but extremely rewarding, is the purple-pink-flowered *A. schubertii*, which bears its great exploding blooms on stems of differing lengths.

The ornamental species are very compliant, but have to be controlled – not only are they self-seeding, they also produce offset bulbs, thus forming large clumps. Ornamental alliums are useful for flower arranging, because their decorative blooms last well in water and, dried, they are a welcome winter addition.

FLOWERING SEASON: From spring through to late autumn.
SOIL CONDITIONS: Fertile soil that drains freely.
SITUATE: In full sunshine.
PROPAGATION: Sow *A. schoenoprasum* in situ at the edges of borders. Plant bulbous varieties at some depth at the end of summer.
RESILIENCE: Mostly hardy.
CARE: Beware of onion fly.

OPPOSITE: The tall stalks of *A. aflatunense* have been underplanted with their smaller cousin, chives (*A. shoenoprsum*), in a clever combination at Loseley Hall Herb Garden in Surrey, England.

Anemone (Ranunculaceae)

anemone

Gently quivering wood anemones (*Anemone nemorosa*) in the pale early-spring sunshine announce the end of winter. Their more sophisticated relatives unfold their delicate petals later in the spring, suffusing the garden with the most beautiful palette of colours.

Known as 'daughter of the wind', the anemone was identified and named by the Greek philosopher Theophrastus in the fourth century BC. It was so named because the wind was said to be responsible for the flowers opening. Today there are about 120 species, which flower from spring to autumn.

The Ancient Greek legend of Aphrodite's love for Adonis tells of her following him in her golden chariot to protect him when hunting. However, he was gored by a huge wild boar, and she arrived in time only to hold him as he died. Some versions say the flowers of *A. coronaria*, the poppy anemone, grew from her tears; others that they sprang from where his blood fell. Yet another legend claims that anemones are also sacred to the Virgin Mary, because they were splashed with Christ's blood on Golgotha.

Poppy anemones, *A. coronaria*, are found from the Mediterranean to central Asia. They were highly prized as long ago as the sixteenth century. There is a tale in Holland of a shameless dignitary trailing his official furred hem through a prized collection to obtain some of the precious seeds. The sixteenth-century herbalist John Gerard claimed 12 different sorts in his garden, but had heard of many more. Several decades later John Parkinson, another renowned herbalist, wrote in his *Paradisus in sole paradisus terrestris* of 1629 that *Anemone coronaria* is 'full of variety and so dainty, so pleasant and so delight some'.

The environs of Caen and Bayeux in Normandy became the epicentre for the cultivation of poppy anemones during the early eighteenth century. In England they were described as one of the chief garden flowers. They were popular with exhibitors and became florists' flowers (see also *Hyacinthus*, page 99 and *Primula auricula*, page 150), but they quickly fell from favour, eventually being abandoned as an exhibition flower by the end of the century.

Varieties of *A. coronaria* were cultivated in Ireland in the 1880s by a Mrs Lawrenson of Dublin, who used St Brigid as her nom de plume, giving rise to the single-flowered St Brigid Group and also the double-flowered De Caen Group anemones. They became popular again, and were being grown commercially as cut flowers by the early twentieth century.

The spring-flowering *A. x fulgens*, a small delicate crimson-flowered beauty used to carpet the vineyards of southern France. It was imported to England in large numbers for enthusiasts in the early nineteenth century, and can still be found. It is well worth searching for.

Another small variety that flowers in early spring, *A. blanda* from Greece and Turkey, is obtainable in shades of white, pink, mauve and blue. This, together with *A. apennina* (which, although usually blue, sometimes has white flowers, some with pink tinges to them), can be happily naturalised in meadows and glades.

Anemones are now widely cultivated as cut flowers and are surprisingly enduring. I was enthralled to find bunches of single colours in a Parisian street market some years ago; they are now sold everywhere in this way.

Most anemones are not difficult to grow in a border. Misfits in the colour scheme can be ruthlessly picked and enjoyed indoors. But nothing can compare with the sight of them blowing freely in the wind that names them, in their natural environment.

ABOVE AND OPPOSITE: Anemones come in an abundant range of colours, from the palest, most delicate whites, to rich red tones.

FLOWER SEASON: Spring to autumn.
SOIL CONDITIONS: Preferred soil conditions vary according to species.
SITUATE: In sun and/or partial shade.
PROPAGATION: Tubers and rhizomes can be planted in the autumn. Sow ripe seed in pots under glass.
RESILIENCE: They are reasonably hardy but autumn-flowering species do not enjoy being frosted.
CARE: Conditions of growth vary for each type so it is a good idea to consult a nurseryman. Watch out for caterpillars, slugs and leaf diseases.

Aquilegia (Ranunculaceae)

columbine

FLOWERING SEASON: Early spring to mid-summer.
SOIL CONDITIONS: Ideally rich soil that is damp, but they are very tolerant plants.
SITUATE: In full sunshine or partial shade..
PROPAGATION: Divide established clumps in spring or autumn. In spring sow seeds in containers under glass. Species tend to hybridise so will not come true from garden-collected seed.
RESILIENCE: Hardy.
CARE: Taller species need staking. Cut back after flowering for a second crop of flowers. Cut back dead stems before winter.

OPPOSITE: In close-up, the intricate structure of the petals of the columbine – four upright petals surrounded by five outer ones – can be seen clearly close up.
BELOW: Columbines form a softening link between other elements in a cottage border.

The gracious bonnets of the aquilegia have brought joy for centuries, populating gardens with ease and lifting the spirits. The most inspiring planting I've seen was in a garden in Australia. Aquilegias, irises and Queen Anne's lace (*Anthriscus sylvestris*) combined to create a cool uplifting sanctuary of whites, pinks and blues – an oasis of tranquillity in the baking heat, surrounded by parched land and gum trees.

Columbine comes from the Latin word *columba*, meaning dove-like, and *aquilegia* from *aquila*, eagle – perhaps because its spur-like petals are talon-shaped. Aquilegias grow wild through most of the temperate northern hemisphere and there are about 70 species of this hardy herbaceous perennial.

The charming flowers of *Aquilegia vulgaris* that decorate the lanes of the West Country of England were being cultivated in gardens by the thirteenth century. It is described in manuscripts and depicted in paintings from the time, planted in the company of violets, roses, lilies and irises around the turf benches of medieval paradise gardens, where it symbolised the dove of peace. This was the only known species then, but it grew in colours of blue, red, purple and white, and some mixed.

Aquilegias were described by John Gerard, an English herbalist of the sixteenth century, as having 'five little hollowe hornes, as it were hanging foorth, with four leaves standing upright as in the shape of little birds'. The columbine was thought in medieval England to be the food of lions, and by rubbing it on one's hand, one assumed the beasts' courage.

The settling of North America produced new species, and *A. canadensis* was thriving in the mid-seventeenth century. With its intense yellow and red spurred petals, it proved very popular in cottage gardens in North America and England during the eighteenth and nineteenth centuries. More varieties had arrived by Victorian times and there were many hybrids. Some of these, examples of which still survive, had long spurs and narrow flowers.

Another American species is *A. caerulea*, which reaches 60cm (24in) and flowers in early summer. It has beautiful pale green foliage, with large long-spurred white flowers that can be tinged with light blue and yellow. There are also red and white examples. *A. longissima* is a real beauty from Mexico. Tall – up to 90cm (36in) – its scented pale yellow flowers again carry long spurs and bloom all summer long if dead-headed. It is one of the founder members of the numerous long-spurred varieties.

The small alpine varieties are generally difficult to grow and should perhaps be left to the specialist. However, in a cool climate, such as Scotland, they can be grown with ease.

Columbines are essential in cottage gardens, their subtle clouds of flowers being a harmonising link between more strident members.

The dominance of the long-spurred varieties is overshadowing the older types, but most varieties have been able to survive the changes in fashion by being exchanged among fellow gardeners. This valuable custom ensures the survival of many enchanting garden flowers for future generations.

Arum (Araceae)

arum lily

The entrancing tender green sheaths of lords and ladies – Britain's native arum lily – seem too delicate to have pushed their way through the cold winter earth. When they emerge they are the softest green, and they bring spring with them. In autumn the sumptuous red berries are held proudly erect and seem to glow from the light undergrowth of the woodland edge. They are often accompanied by red-and-white-spotted fly agaric mushrooms, for they both love dank forest glades.

The plants have long been associated with fertility and lust: even the Latin name, *Arum maculatum* was dictated by the very masculine form that this flower takes. However, it does have more genteel local names such as 'priest-in-the-pulpit', which refers to the contrast between the two parts of the flower – the upright spadix or 'priest' and the encircling sheath or pulpit.

The sixteenth-century Unicorn Tapestries that decorate the Cloisters in New York, a branch of the Metropolitan Museum of Art, contain examples of *A. maculatum*. This famous tapestry, which tells the tale of the capture of the unicorn, depicts it chained to a pomegranate tree – itself a symbol of fertility – and surrounded by the herbs associated with venery, including *Persicaria bistorta* or snakeweed and bluebells *(Hyacinthoides non-scripta)*. Bluebells are linked with Selene, the moon goddess who fell in love with the shepherd Endymion, according to Greek legend. She made him sleep for ever so

that she could caress him every night. Snakeweed is another phallic-looking plant. In folklore arums brought into the house invited certain doom, perhaps because of the symbolism of sexuality mixed with religion.

Most of the 26 species of arum have been used as a source of both food and medicine. For instance, *A. italicum*, which is widespread in temperate climates, was eaten by the Ancient Greeks who salted the leaves and ate them. They considered the root mixed with bullocks' dung a good remedy for gout. Dioscorides, the renowned Greek physician of this time, recommended rubbing one's hands with the root to deter vipers.

A. maculatum was also eaten in medieval times because it was considered health-giving. Taken in large quantities, however, it was thought to terminate pregnancy. The powdered root was once used to make Portland arrowroot, a substitute for genuine arrowroot from the West Indies. It was also more commonly used as a starch for laundering linen, though many a washerwoman had her hands blistered and covered in sores by this harsh substance.

The most extraordinary member of this family is *Dracunculus vulgaris*, the dragon arum. It grows in the Mediterranean in rocky terrain, and bears striking flowers of the deepest velvety chocolate-purple, which can measure up to a metre in length, with a thick spadix of the same colour. It is like lords and ladies on steroids, and emits a foul odour of putrescence. The plant has

made an impression on people throughout the centuries. For instance, it is depicted on a late Minoan sarcophagus *c.*1460 BC now in the museum at Heraklion in Crete. Dioscorides, in Ancient Greece, observed that if a decoction of the plant was drunk with wine it stirred up the 'vehement desires to conjunction'. An aphrodisiac not to be trifled with.

In Crete one spring I noticed that unusual weather conditions had made the dragonas, as the dragon arum is called there, proliferate. It was the most amazing sight. Old ladies picked them by the armful, perhaps an inherited memory of some pagan rite. We gathered some to photograph. When we had finished I stood them in the courtyard, where they attracted every fly from miles around. Fortunately the flies stayed in the courtyard with the flowers and ignored the house completely.

The dragon arum will grow in a sheltered site in cooler climates, and it is well worth an attempt, for it is the most sensuously exotic creature to behold. A real talking point.

SOIL CONDITIONS: Garden arums like damp soil.
SITUATE: Garden arums like partial shade, dragon arums prefer full sun.
PROPAGATION: Tubers should be planted in summer, or late spring for the dragon arum. *Arum maculatum* self-seeds readily once established.
RESILIENCE: Dragon arums are not fully hardy.
CARE: Top dress in autumn and add a covering of straw or horticultural fleece to dragon arums.

OPPOSITE: The beautiful (but foul-smelling) *Dracunculus vulgaris*, also known as the dragonas of Crete.

Calendula (Compositae)

marigold
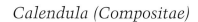

The joyful flowers of the bright marigold open and close with the rising and setting sun. They are borne in profusion throughout the summer and even survive into winter, if it is mild. The colours range from pale yellow to the darkest orange – some, such as the regal 'Indian Prince', even tinged with brown. These amenable plants will take care of themselves and make glowing members of informal gardens.

The marigold was given its botanical name, calendula, because it was believed to flower on the 'calends' – the first day of every month. It was also dedicated to the Virgin Mary (hence its common name Mary-gold), and it is in flower for all her devotional festivals.

Marigolds have a long history of cultivation, probably because they are prolific, floriferous and have many medicinal and culinary uses. In the kitchen marigolds were used as a cheap substitute for saffron. Although lacking in flavour, they coloured butter and were even used as a yellow hair dye. The leaves were also used to flavour soups and stews, hence the name pot marigold.

SOIL CONDITIONS: Grows best in poor soil.
SITUATE: In sun or light shade.
PROPAGATION: Sow directly in the garden in spring, then again in summer. Will self-seed readily.
RESILIENCE: Hardy annual.
CARE: Watch out for greenfly. Powdery mildew can be a problem in dry weather.

OPPOSITE The familiar faces of the pot marigold (*Calendula officinalis*).

It was believed that marigolds picked at dusk on Midsummer day would resolve a lover's tiff, and sowing marigold seeds in a lover's footprints was supposed to keep him faithful.

In the Middle Ages marigolds were deemed to be useful as a treatment for insect and snake bites if laid on the wounds. When taken internally they were said to have healing properties for the intestines and liver.

By the seventeenth century the marigold had reached North America, and it later proved invaluable during the Civil War as it was gathered by doctors to treat open wounds. Marigolds are still used by herbalists of today to alleviate respiratory ailments and skin problems.

In the kitchen garden marigolds make a marvellous edging for a plot of yellow vegetables. Imagine their golden blooms outlining a bed of yellow courgettes, golden haricot beans and tiny golden-yellow tomatoes.

The marigold also proves a good companion plant by discouraging blackfly and attracting the hoverfly, the larvae of which consume greenfly voraciously. Companion planting was used long before the introduction of pesticides and is a useful tactic in the strategy of gardeners who wish to avoid using chemicals.

Marigolds love long hot summers, when they spread and self-seed, invading gravel paths and barren patches. If you allow for this attribute when planning your garden it can be a blessing rather than a curse.

They are long-lasting as cut flowers and their pungent blooms bring bursts of sunshine into the room, and smiles to faces.

Campanula (Ranunculaceae)

bell flower

The genus *Campanula* includes a number of native flowers, each with its particular traditions and folklore. The enchanting harebell, *Campanula rotundifolia*, with its dainty blue flowers that dance in the zephyrs of summer, is sadly disappearing from the countryside in England with the ever-encroaching spread of urban life. We prize the flowers, yet in medieval times the harebell was also known as devil's bell, witch bell and witch thimble, and was not picked, for bad luck would follow. It has been recorded in all the well-known reference books from that of John Gerard, the sixteenth-century herbalist, onwards. He called harebells both Coventry bells and Canterbury bells.

The only medicinal use for plants in this genus seems to have been a decoction of *C. trachelium*, once known as throatwort. It was recommended as a healing gargle or mouthwash by Gerard. At this time the shoots of the giant throatwort, *C. latifolia*, were considered edible and used as a substitute for spinach.

True Canterbury bells, *C. medium*, were grown in medieval gardens. They were looked upon as rather humble, but as more sophisticated forms were bred they grew in status. The single species were superseded by doubles, and the blue forms were joined by both pink and white varieties.

Most campanula species hail from the Caucasus, Greece or northern Europe, but some are native to many other parts of the world, including the Atlas Mountains of Morocco, Japan and North America. They are a mixed bag, and there was a lot of campanula confusion

until Linnaeus sorted things out with his *Genera Plantarum* in 1737 the basis of modern botanical classification. By 1786 plant hunters had identified more than 2,000 species.

Campanulas are amiable plants and easily cultivated. With species ranging from tiny alpines to spires of flowers that reach great heights, the choice is vast. Even the alpines are easy to grow, and species with a creeping habit are useful for filling gaps.

Campanulas have two quite distinct flower shapes: stars and bells. The dwarf perennial *C. garganica* from Greece is of the former group,

covered with star-shaped blue flowers from early to late summer. The perennial *C. carpatica*, from the Carpathian Mountains, is a good example of the bell-shaped form. Small and growing in clumps, it bears cupped flowers ranging from blue through to purple. Of the large varieties the chimney bellflower *C. pyramidalis* can reach great heights, though it is short-lived. In Victorian times it was sometimes grown as a house plant and trained over fans of wire to form a living net curtain at the window – a technique that sounds as if it could be worth reviving.

SOIL CONDITIONS: Prefer well-drained fertile soil.
SITUATE: Sunny position – some species like light shade.
PROPAGATION: Sow seed in autumn or spring, depending on species. Divide clumps of perennials in spring.
RESILIENCE: Hardy, though some alpines dislike heavy winter rain.
CARE: Slugs and snails may feast on tender new shoots. Rust can be a problem.

LEFT AND OPPOSITE: *Campanula persificolia*, whether in white or purple, makes a useful plant in a mixed border.

Cerinthe (Boraginaceae)

cerinthe

The cerinthe is a wildflower native to south-eastern Europe. It is a small, pretty annual whose delicate foliage makes it very effective in a border and well worth growing, especially if you wish to attract bees. Its flowers are full of nectar, hence its common name honeywort. *Cerinthe major* has drooping flowers that are usually yellow with brown at their base. *C. retorta* has yellow-and violet-tipped flowers surrounded by violet bracts.

Dioscorides. a physician of Ancient Greece, advised the use of the compressed leaves of *C. major* to remove white spots from nails, and applied after vinegar they were supposed to do the same for white blotches on the skin. I first saw these plants growing in the garden of the Mediterranean Garden Society at Peonia near Athens, whose dedicated members are keen to preserve for the future the indigenous plants of the Mediterranean. Happily, I have since seen it grown in gardens in England.

SOIL CONDITIONS: Grows best in poor soil.
SITUATE: In sun or light shade.
PROPAGATION: Sow directly in the garden in spring, then again in summer. Will self-seed readily.
RESILIENCE: Hardy annual.
CARE: Watch out for greenfly.

BELOW: The subtle flowers of *Cerinthe major* give no hint that they are particularly rich in nectar.
Opposite: *C. major purpurascens* is an unusual but easy-to-grow annual for any garden.

Chrysanthemum (Asteraceae)

chrysanthemum

The extravagant heads of chrysanthemums have been an inspiration for generations of gardeners and flower lovers alike. They are simply too good to be true. Peer into one of the huge perfect white puffs of a bloom and see how many shades of white can be found in a single flower. The shining bronze beauties that seem to radiate warmth are equally impressive, while the velvety reds offer depths of colour that are all the more welcome because chrysanthemums flower at the time of year when gardens begin to look a little tired. They will go on flowering until the first hard frosts, or longer under glass, of course. For me their pungent leaves are particularly evocative – a scent that's inseparable from their stunning flowers.

The chrysanthemum has been grown in China for the past 2,500 years, where it is deeply revered and depicted on porcelain and in paintings. It was introduced to Japan in about the ninth century and was adapted as the symbol of the Emperor.

The name chrysanthemum is derived from the Greek words *chrysos*, meaning gold, and *anthos*, a flower. The large-flowered form was introduced to Holland at the end of the seventeenth century, and by the early nineteenth century varieties had arrived in Britain from China, causing huge interest among the wealthy. At the same time chrysanthemums from Japan were sent to Boston and from there were exported to Britain. Crossing two species (*Chrysanthemum. sinesis and C. indicum*) gave rise to the vast choice of varieties available today. There are tall and dwarf varieties, discreet singles and the great blowsy beauties beloved of exhibitors. Prizes for the finest blooms are hotly contested at local flower shows.

The rather artificial-looking sprays sold all year round as cut flowers, although long-lasting are poor examples of these beautiful blooms. It is worth searching for more unusual types, which will reward you with a blaze of russet and bronze heads glowing in the autumn sunshine.

FLOWERING SEASON: Those categorised as 'early' flower from late summer to early autumn; 'mid-season' in mid-autumn; and 'late' mid-autumn to mid-winter. Both early and late-flowering varieties are not fully hardy and must be moved under glass in autumn, in cold climates.

SOIL CONDITIONS: Fertile neutral to slightly acid soil with good humus content.

SITUATE: In full sun but sheltered from the elements.

PROPAGATION: Sow seed in spring or autumn directly in the garden. Take cuttings in spring or divide established clumps in spring or early autumn.

RESILIENCE: Hardy to frost-tender.

CARE: Water freely in dry weather and apply a liquid feed until buds show colour. Protect with a mulch in winter and cut back in early spring. Watch out for common pests and diseases.

THIS PAGE: The ethereally pale petals of *Chrysanthemum* 'Pavilion'.

Clematis (Ranunculaceae)

clematis

The sight of blue star-shaped clematis flowers, perhaps *Clematis* 'Beauty of Worcester', intermingling with the gentle pink of a musk rose, is one of the glories of an early summer garden. Scrambling happily towards the light, the clematis needs support, but this can be easily provided. It scales trellis, shrubs and trees; mixes beautifully with roses and blossom; and twines itself around gateposts and pergolas; and clambers over tree stumps and old buildings.

There are varieties that flower in spring, summer and autumn in a diverse range of colours, from white, palest lemons, pinks and blues to deepest purple. Clematis present a unique opportunity for creativity throughout the year if chosen carefully.

Although full of character, the humble native clematis that decorates the hedgerows and byways of rural Britain has rarely been featured either in art or literature, perhaps because it is so commonplace. It remained anonymous until the sixteenth century, when C. *vitalba* was first mentioned by William Turner in his Names of Herbes published in 1551. He referred to it as the hedge vine. Later John Gerard, the English herbalist, described it in his *Herball* of 1591 as 'making a goodly shadow, thereupon I have named it Travellers' Joy'.

The name clematis is derived from the Greek word *klematis*, a diminutive of *klema* that means vine, branch or twig. Local names for the native British species include old man's beard, often attributed to the fact that it bears long feathery seedheads. However, 'old man' in folklore can also mean the devil, hence its other local names of devil's twister and devil's guts. Other members of the genus have common names such as virgin's bower and ladies bower, either in homage to Queen Elizabeth I or dedicated to the Virgin Mary, so the clematis seems to have a foot firmly in both camps.

Clematis does have some practical uses. For example, the Greek physician Dioscorides recommended beating the seeds in water, which 'drives down phlegm and choler... the leaves being laid down removes leprosies'. In the past clematis vines were woven into the bottom of crab pots, because they are both flexible and durable. Today the same properties make clematis prunings useful for shaping into wreath bases. And for centuries the hollow stems were smoked (usually a pastime for young boys), causing it to be called whiffy-cane, gipsy's-bacca and numerous other local names.

The first foreign species, *C. viticella*, arrived from Spain in 1569 and was known as the purple virgin's bower. The reign of Elizabeth I saw many arrivals from Europe, notably the winter-flowering *C. cirrhosa* and *C. flammula*, which bears fragrant white flowers in autumn. In the early eighteenth century some native North

OPPOSITE: The bold flowers of *Clematis* 'Jubilee'.
LEFT: Clematis and roses make a traditional combination that still looks good in gardens today.
ABOVE: A glorious soft pink clematis that is almost translucent.

American species were introduced, including *C. crispa*, the marsh clematis from the south, and *C. viorna*, the leather flower, from the east.

The opening up of the Far East – Japan was effectively closed to the West until the mid-nineteenth century – created a frenzy of plant collecting, resulting in many species arriving from Korea, China and Japan. This plunder continued unabated until the First World War. During the war growers in Britain busied themselves by breeding and hybridising, producing the glorious range of large-flowered hybrids available today.

The range of varieties on offer peaked between the Wars, when more than 300 were available to the public. Sadly, many of these have now disappeared as the enthusiasm for clematis waned.

In recent years, however, the interest in this climber has revived and many more new varieties with exciting colours and a good growing habit are now being introduced.

The clematis thrives in mixed company. It will grow in pots if the roots are kept cool by underplanting, but it comes into its own as it adorns vertical structures, walkways and even trees with its swags and garlands. Some varieties are highly scented; seek these out if perfume is a priority, but mixed with roses, honeysuckle and other scented climbers this is not a necessity – concentrate instead on form and colour. Select varieties carefully by visiting nurseries through the seasons: look at foliage and fruits, as well as flowers, then their beauty can be enjoyed for most of the gardening year.

FLOWERING SEASON: Different varieties flower through the seasons.
SOIL CONDITIONS: Rich free-draining soil.
SITUATE: In full sunlight or partial shade but protect the roots from the sun.
PROPAGATION: Sow seed when ripe under glass, but it won't always come true. Layering is an easier way to increase stocks.
RESILIENCE: Hardy to slightly frost-prone.
CARE: Support young plants until they are established. Mulch with well-rotted manure or compost in winter. Prune late-flowering clematis in winter for maximum flowers. Others need little pruning, except to shape or tidy them. Wilt – caused by a fungus – affects large-flowered clematis. Planting them deeply encourages extra shoots, to increase chances of survival.

ABOVE: A collection of clematis includes the wine-coloured *C.* 'Jubileinyizo' (top right), the lilac *C.* 'Teschio' (bottom right), the pale pink *C.* 'Peveril Pearl' (bottom centre) and the frilly *C.* 'Veronicas's Choice' (bottom left).

Cleome (Capparaceae)

spider flower

The long stamens of the cleome or spider flower give this plant a unique appearance. Close inspection reveals great choruses of flowers; viewed from afar, they coalesce into imposing spires that rival delphiniums in height. It is one of those plants that make you realise the amazing diversity of shape and colour that abounds in the garden. Truly inspirational, the cleome stirs creative urges to paint, to photograph, to embroider and above all, to enjoy all the garden treasures we possess.

Of the 150 species that are native to the mountainous valleys and plains of sub-tropical and tropical regions of the world, only one is commonly cultivated in Britain. The genus includes shrubby deciduous varieties, but it is the bushy annual, *Cleome hassleriana* from South America, that is grown in gardens. It has highly perfumed flowers of white, pink or purple, flowering into autumn if dead-headed regularly and there are no early frosts.

The spider flower is a tall plant, reaching 1.5m (5ft) and makes a useful filler for larger borders. From a distance, and before the flowers are fully opened, it can be mistaken for a phlox; up close, the impossibly long stamens can be seen unfolding, like a harvest spider's legs. Search out the variety 'Colour Fountain', a little shorter than the species, with blooms up to 10cm (4in) across, in various shade of pink and whites.

Certain gardeners are prejudiced against annuals and don't consider them serious garden plants. Not Marylyn Abbott, who is restoring the garden at West Green House in Hampshire, England. Being Australian, she is not hidebound by the strictures of the English gardener and is willing to try all sorts of plants. She uses cleomes as fillers in her herbaceous borders, planting them with delphiniums and phlox, for example, where they create a mist of colour. In late summer the garden is a feast of well-chosen colour schemes and amply repays visiting for its inspirational ideas and interesting plant combinations.

FLOWERING SEASON: Summer flowering.
SOIL CONDITIONS: Plant in light sandy fertile soil.
SITUATE: In full sunlight.
PROPAGATION: Sow seeds under glass in spring, planting out when the danger of frost has passed.
RESILIENCE: Half-hardy.
CARE: Keep well watered and apply a balanced feed every month during the growing season. Dead-head to prolong flowering. Watch out for aphids.

BELOW: *Cleome hassleriana* 'Colour Fountain' bears its strongly scented flowers in summer.

Clivia (Amaryllidaceae)

clivia

The hot shimmering colours of clivias are almost tangible – especially in the lengthening evening shadows, when their waxy flowers start to glow. In colours with the intensity of velvet, the flowers surmount fountains of dark green leaves that fade into the twilight. They bring the aura of sultry evenings, just before the stars emerge and the earth cools.

Clivias were named after Lady Charlotte Clive, who was married to the third Duke of Northumberland and died in 1866. The plants hail from South Africa and, with many other new arrivals from the Cape in the mid-nineteenth century, became popular with wealthy owners of hot-houses.

In areas that are prone to frost they are best grown in a greenhouse or conservatory kept at a minimum of 10°C (50°F), or even as an impressive house plant. Their dark green strap-shaped evergreen leaves have a beauty all of their own when the flowers have faded. Clivias bloom from spring to summer in the most glorious colours: bright pinks, reds, oranges and yellows. If grown in containers they can go outside in summer to add great splashes of colour to a terrace or patio. I think the best species is *Clivia miniata*, which bears bright red or orange trumpet-shaped flowers, each with a yellow throat.

In Australia clivias are grown with ease as container specimens, in great glowing banks or as colourful additions to a border. They have such a lush appearance that it is easy to forget the constant battle necessary to preserve the garden oases of Australia. Drought looms large and most keen gardeners have a catchment dam that supplies water for the garden. Yet the soft, almost English-style gardens of the Blue Mountains and Southern Highlands are necessary havens where their creators can escape the rugged realities that lie beyond.

FLOWERING SEASON: From spring to summer.
SOIL CONDITIONS: Fertile free-draining soil enriched with humus. Under glass grow in potting compost with a loam content.
SITUATE: They like some shade.
PROPAGATION: Divide established clumps in late winter or spring. Sow seed in spring, in a propagator.
RESILIENCE: Susceptible to frost.
CARE: Potted plants benefit from liquid feed; water less in winter. Clivias enjoy being pot-bound and dislike being disturbed.

OPPOSITE: A stunning container-grown specimen of *Clivia miniata* at Fern Brook in the Blue Mountains of New South Wales, Australia.

Convallaria (Liliaceae)

lily-of-the-valley

The delicate white bells of the lily-of-the-valley are the epitome of simple pure beauty. Its soft green leaves pierce the earth in early spring, unfurling to reveal a small spire of the most exquisitely perfumed perfect flowers. Their fragrance alone could melt the hardest heart.

Named from the Latin *convallis*, meaning valley, the lily-of-the-valley is a perennial of deciduous woodlands in the British Isles, Europe, temperate Asia and North America. It has many local names, among them May lilies, fairies bells, innocents and ladies tears.

Lily-of-the-valley is steeped in folklore. German legend has it that it grew from the tears of the Virgin Mary at the foot of the Cross. Lady chapels and statues of the Virgin Mary were adorned with these delicate bells throughout Europe in the Middle Ages.

The flowers distilled in either water or brandy were used to cure fainting, hysteria and headaches until Regency times. Its leaves were also laid on wounds and grazes. The plant is still used in medicine today, having properties akin to *Digitalis* (see page 60). However, it is toxic, so should not be used in home remedies. Lily-of-the-valley is much used by parfumiers, too.

In the garden, lily-of-the-valley is beautiful when naturalised in copses and woodland. The foliage makes excellent ground cover, even in dark difficult corners. The plants grow happily in terracotta pots and can be encouraged to bloom early, making the most delightful house plants in spring. For the florist they are an essential ingredient of posies, and are a traditional element of bridal bouquets.

FLOWERING SEASON: Spring.
SOIL CONDITIONS: Fertile moist soil enriched with humus.
SITUATE: They prefer the shade but will tolerate sunshine.
PROPAGATION: Sow ripe seed after removing fleshy coating. Divide large clumps in winter.
RESILIENCE: Hardy.
CARE: At the beginning of winter lift rhizomes and set in pots for early flowering house plants. Generally self-sufficient.

OPPOSITE: The familiar nodding heads of *Convallaria majalis* have had a host of uses throughout the years, from perfume to bridal bouquets.

Cosmos (Asteraceae)

COSMOS

The delicate cosmos, with its soft foliage, looks particularly beautiful sparkling with raindrops in the incandescent light that follows a storm. Surprisingly resilient for a plant of such apparent fragility, its velvety petals cup teardrops that gleam in the pale blue light.

It seems entirely appropriate that its name comes from the Greek *kosmos*, meaning beautiful. The genus contains about 25 species of annuals and perennials native to the rough pasture and fields of Central America and the southern USA.

The plants are relatively new to the gardens of Europe. *Cosmos astrosanguineus* arrived in Britain in 1835, when William Thompson of Ipswich had seeds sent to him from Mexico. It is a perennial that bears blooms of the deepest brownish-maroon from mid-summer onwards, smelling, astonishingly, of chocolate.

C. bipinnatus is a delightful annual that has large flowers in white, pink or crimson, with bright yellow centres. If dead-headed it will flower all summer, making it a hardworking ingredient in a mixed or perennial border. The flowerheads dance among the feathery foliage, adding a dimension of softness and movement to the planting. They even seed themselves if left to their own devices. This species is also worth growing in pots or in rows in a cutting bed to provide flowers for the home. They look equally attractive in both the large formal garden and the friendly cottage garden. They are used with great success at Villandry in the Loire Valley in France, where they are grown in the fountain garden among clipped evergreens.

I have also seen cosmos used spectacularly at the Prieuré Notre Dame d'Orsan in the Berry region of France. This reconstruction of a medieval garden has been enlivened by bending the rules a little, rather than creating a slavish reproduction, and these gentle flowers are a joy to behold there.

FLOWERING SEASON: All summer and into early autumn.
SOIL CONDITIONS: Rich moist soil that is free-draining.
SITUATE: In full sunshine.
PROPAGATION: If grown in pots, sow in early spring. Sow directly in the garden during late spring.
RESILIENCE: Hardy and semi-hardy species.
CARE: Dead-head for a longer flowering season, leaving some to self-seed. Aphids and slugs love them. Lift half-hardy perennials in frost-prone areas.

ABOVE: The rich tones of *C. bipinnatus* 'Sea Shells'.
OPPOSITE: The feathery foliage and delicate flowers of cosmos look stunning in the sunshine in the gardens of Château Villandry, France.

The fiery arcs of the crocosmia or montbretia rise like fireworks above elegant tapering leaves. Visit a garden while they are in flower and you will be drawn to these colourful magnets. They sing out at the height of summer when a host of other border beauties are vying for attention and their graceful dignified form has an exquisite charm all of its own.

Crocosmia takes its name from the Greek *krokos*, meaning saffron, and *osme*, smell. Intriguingly the flowers have no scent when growing, but dried and subsequently steeped in water they develop the perfume of the crocus.

Modern montbretias are derived from two closely related plants, tritonia and crocosmia, both native to South Africa. Montbretias were named after Antoine François Ernest Conquebert de Montbret, one of a group of botanists who went with Napoleon to Africa in 1798. But Nelson destroyed the French fleet, Napoleon fled and the botanists were stranded. Eventually they were allowed home to France, bringing with them the plant specimens they had collected.

FLOWERING SEASON: Throughout summer into early autumn.
SOIL CONDITIONS: Humus-enriched soil that drains freely.
SITUATE: They thrive in full sunlight but also enjoy some shade.
PROPAGATION: Sow ripe seed in pots under glass. Lift and divide established clumps in spring.
RESILIENCE: Hardy but they dislike prolonged frost.
CARE: Protect with a mulch in their first winter of growth and also if there is a continuing frost. Watch out for spider mites.

Crocosmia (Iridaceae)

montbretia

Crocosmia were discovered in South Africa by the eccentric English plant collector William Burchell. Having trained at Kew, he set off in 1810 to explore South Africa in a covered ox-cart, with Union Jack aloft. He entertained the locals with his flute and travelled unharmed in even the wildest regions. Victor Lemoine, the famous French plant breeder, crossed tritonia and crocosmia in the late nineteenth century and from then on the montbretia has been a popular garden addition.

The flowers range from a pale yellow, through the oranges, to a bright tomato-red. *Crocosmia masoniorum* has soft green leaves that appear to be pleated, and bears orange-red flowers in mid-summer. The popular variety *C.* 'Lucifer' is similar, but has flowers that look upwards, and are of the brightest red. They can be planted with panache in fashionable 'hot' borders, alongside exotic cannas and fiery dahlias. They lend an elegant tracery to the borders with their knife-like foliage breaking up the colours.

Almost every cottage garden has a clump of montbretias somewhere, for they are hardy and long-lived. I inherited a bed of them in the Norfolk garden that sparked my journey of discovery. They had obviously been there for years. Their jolly flowers lit up a rather dark corner, the mixture of orange flowers glowing against green tapering leaves enhancing the warm red of the local brickwork.

LEFT AND RIGHT: The boldly coloured blooms of montbretia, from yellow through to the brightest red, have a structural quality when examined in detail.

Cyclamen (Primulaceae)

cyclamen

The sweet swept-back petals of the cyclamen are reminiscent of a ballerina with her skirts held aloft. Their purity of colour is intense and their simple foliage makes a perfect foil to their floral beauty. The name cyclamen comes from the Greek word for circle, *kuklos*, and the Ancient Greeks knew it as *chelonion*, or little tortoise, to which they likened its corm.

Over the centuries the cyclamen has had many medicinal applications. The Greek philosopher Theophrastus suggested using it to heal wounds and boils. During the Renaissance, when it was believed that like healed like, the ear-shaped leaves of the plant were supposed to indicate that it could cure earache. In England in the late sixteenth century, cyclamen was used to induce childbirth, it was deemed so potent that pregnant women were advised to avoid it at all costs, until needed. John Gerard, a herbalist of the period, grew *Cyclamen neapolitanum* and *C. coum* and noted that the latter could be seen growing wild in some parts of the country. However, the general consensus now is that the plants had escaped from gardens.

Another name for cyclamen is sow-bread, as the corms were fed to pigs in the Perigord area of France, to enhance the flavour of the pork. Mrs Beeton, Victorian doyenne of cookery and domestic matters, made a point of recommending delicacies from this area.

About 17 species of cyclamen are native to a wide range of terrains from the Mediterranean, east to Iran and encompassing Russia. The large hot-house cyclamens available from most garden centres and florists today are derived from *C. persicum*, which in fact hails from

Syria, not Persia. Nurserymen in the Victorian era selected the biggest plants and raised them from their seed.

By far the most attractive species to grow are the delicate garden varieties, which are either spring or autumn flowering. They will naturalise under trees, where their enchantingly swept-back petals in the softest pinks and whites nestle happily among the tree roots. They do equally well in rock gardens.

As recently as the 1970s the demand for these plants was such that they were plundered from their native lands. The World Conservation Union has launched an international programme to protect threatened species like the cyclamen, but some illegally dug plants still slip through the net. These are most likely to be sold as dried tubers; buying plants from an established nursery will help stamp out this trade.

To come across cyclamen in their native environment is like discovering rare gems. After scrambling up the rather difficult mountainsides of Crete in spring, I have been rewarded by great clusters of *C. creticum*. Its small, scented white flowers are like stars against the dark green of its foliage. It flourishes here in the stony damp meadows of the mountains and, fortunately, is left in peace.

FLOWERING SEASON: All year, depending on species.
SOIL CONDITIONS: Fairly rich soil with high humus content that drains freely.
SITUATE: In dappled shade beneath shrubs and trees.
PROPAGATION: Soak ripe seeds for 12 hours before sowing. Keep in dark until germinated.
RESILIENCE: Most are hardy, except for pot plants.
CARE: Outdoors mulch each year with leafmould when leaves have died back. Pot plants need a cool draught-free spot. Water them from below and feed sparingly with a liquid low-nitrogen feed. Watch out for grey mould.

OPPOSITE: Large pot-grown cultivars of cyclamen are popular at Christmas and on Mothering Sunday, but they can be short-lived.

Cynara scolymus (Asteraceae)
globe artichoke

FLOWERING SEASON: Summer through to autumn.
SOIL CONDITIONS: Rich soil that drains freely.
SITUATE: In full sunshine, sheltered from the wind.
PROPAGATION: Sow seed in pots under glass in spring or take root cuttings in spring or autumn.
RESILIENCE: Hardy, but give extra protection from frost.
CARE: In winter protect roots with a dry mulch. Watch out for aphids and slugs, which adore them.

BELOW: Globe artichokes are well worth the space they take up in the vegetable plot.
OPPOSITE: Close-up, the pink flowers of *Cynara scolymus* look more furry than spiky.

The spectacular globe artichoke, *Cynara scolymus*, is an ideal plant, for not only is it extremely handsome, it is also delicious. The Ancient Egyptians were the first to cultivate the globe artichoke, the Arabs introduced it to Spain and Italy in the fifteenth century, and by the sixteenth century, it was being grown in France and England.

Medicinally the plant is thought to be beneficial for the liver and kidneys. The most effective parts of the plant are said to be the leaves and roots, which are extremely bitter – unlike the delicious buds.

The great dilemma with artichokes is whether to pick and eat them or leave them in all their magnificent glory – their great pointed scrolling leaves surmounted by the sculptural thistles that gradually open to show the rich purple flowers within. I used to do both.

I have two painful gardening memories of artichokes. I had a jobbing gardener who had never encountered these giants, and emerged triumphantly from the kitchen garden once to announce that he had got rid of 'they great sowthistles' for me. My other moment came when entertaining some gourmets to lunch. I picked my first enormous artichokes, of which I was very proud. I was completely unaware that the organically grown artichoke is earwig heaven. Much to my chagrin, we had to wipe each leaf with a napkin before dipping it in melted butter. After this my artichokes sat in salted water for some time before cooking.

The globe artichoke is closely related to the cardoon (*C. cardunculus*), which is equally useful as a vegetable and a garden flower. The young shoots of cardoons are blanched under forcing pots before harvesting, so you must decide early on whether you will eat them or grow them for their flowers. Of the two plants the cardoon has the most handsome foliage and, despite its appearance, is not prickly. They both like a sunny well-drained site and each plant needs at least a square metre of land. Make room for these noble beauties in a mixed border or in a vegetable plot.

Dahlia (Asteraceae)

dahlia

The dahlia, newly reinstated in the fashionable garden, is glorious in all its diverse shapes and sizes. Great bursts of colour shout at you from the border, while smaller, more delicate forms please the eye. Dahlias flower from mid-summer until the first frosts, filling the late-summer gap that besets many garden displays with colours to suit any taste, from the purest white to the darkest velvety red. They are suitable for master plantings or edging a border; plant them 'en masse' in great singing bunches to enhance colour schemes or grow the smaller delicate examples at the front of the border. You can plant them with panache in containers. They make long-lasting cut flowers and look wonderful in cutting beds.

Natives of Mexico and Central America, dahlias were grown by the Aztecs, who reputedly ate the tubers. The Spanish sent them back to the Old World, but they weren't immediately popular – opinions differed on their flavour and their palatability.

Dahlias finally began to be appreciated for their flowers in Europe in the late eighteenth century. They were named after Dr Anders Dahl, who was both a physician and a pupil of Linnaeus. For a while they were also known as georginas after Johann Georgi, a botanist from St Petersburg, but this name has fallen out of use.

By the early nineteenth century new hybrids were being developed in France and the popularity of the dahlia took off. In the 1830s there were almost 1,000 varieties available, most double, but the original single forms remained popular. Dahlia societies soon blossomed and shows and exhibitions were held, with large sums of money offered as prizes for the best blooms. The Victorians planted them in their bouquet gardens, which were great sumptuous displays, while exhibitors planted them in soldierly rows as specimens. Dahlias even became an ingredient of cottage gardens.

As often happens with a fashionable flower, one minute it is the flower of all flowers, then just as swiftly it falls from grace. In the late nineteenth century, double varieties were considered too vulgar and dropped from favour, though single varieties and new cactus-flowered types were spared criticism. Today dahlias have caught the imagination of a new generation of gardeners keen to create bold and colourful herbaceous borders.

FLOWERING SEASON: From early summer through to autumn.
SOIL CONDITIONS: Soil with a high humus content.
SITUATE: In full sun.
PROPAGATION: Bedding plants should be sown under glass in spring. Plant in the garden when frosts are over. Start tubers in early spring under glass, divide into sections, each with a plump bud, and plant out after frosts.
RESILIENCE: Frost-tender.
CARE: As with most plants, dead-heading prolongs flowering. Stake taller examples. Feed weekly in early summer with fertiliser with a high nitrogen content. Cut back after flowering, dig up the tubers and store in a dry place protected from frost. They can be left in situ in areas that are not prone to frost.

Delphinium (Ranunculaceae)

delphinium

The delphinium must be the quintessential plant of the herbaceous border. Its misty colours highlight and accentuate the verticals, while the noble spires, rising above a bed of soft foliage, add style and grace. To look their best, delphiniums need a plain backdrop such as a mellow brick wall, or perhaps a hedge of the deepest velvety green.

As a small child, raised on A. A. Milne, I would search hopefully at their feet for the fabled dormouse:

'There once was a Dormouse who lived in a bed, Of delphiniums (blue) and geraniums (red), And all day long he'd a wonderful view, Of geraniums (red) and delphiniums (blue).'

Perhaps this is why the flowers are especially dear to me. I have always managed to grow them somewhere. Even in large pots, underplanted with soft blowsy pinks, they represent the essence of an English summer, captured in the smallest space imaginable.

The name delphinium is derived from the Greek *delphinion* or dolphin-like, because the spurs on the flowers can resemble a dolphin's snout. Delphiniums are found in mountainous regions worldwide, apart from the Arctic, Antarctic and Australia.

They were known to the Ancient Greeks, and the physician Dioscorides recommended the seeds as an antidote to the sting of a scorpion. He also noted that scorpions themselves were deterred by the plants being strewn about. I must try this method to discourage the small,

ever-present but evasive colony that inhabits the hearth of our little house in Crete.

Closely related larkspur (*Consolida ajacus*), known to some as louse-grass, comes from the Mediterranean, where it has long been used as an insecticide. The seeds, made into a decoction, were said to be an invaluable remedy for infestations of headlice. This annual species is the oldest garden delphinium and it has been grown since the fifteenth century, probably for these very properties.

These older annual species have now been regrouped under the genus *Consolida* rather than *Delphinium*.

In the sixteenth century both Gerard and Parkinson grew *Delphinium elatum* and produced plants with double flowers. The species is one of the forebears of the delphiniums that we know in contemporary gardens.

Many new species were discovered in America and China in the early nineteenth century, and these were crossed with existing plants, resulting in many beautiful tall hybrids. There were both single and double varieties, but the doubles were by far the rarest. At their peak, the popularity of delphiniums was such that in 1910 the renowned nurseryman Amos Perry exhibited a mindboggling 30,000 spires, which must have been an awesome sight. But there would have been no pink varieties among them, for these are a recent innovation, dating from the mid-twentieth century.

Delphiniums are divided into two main groups: those with branching flowerspikes are in the Belladonna Group, those that produce spires of tightly packed blooms are in the Elatum Group. Belladonna delphiniums are all medium height and flower from early to late summer, while those in the Elatum Group flower from

LEFT: The blowsy petals of *D.* 'Bruce'.
OPPOSITE: The vertical spires of delphinium contrast effectively with the rounded forms of trees in the background in a well-established herbaceous border.

early to mid-summer with small, medium and large examples available. There is a third and much smaller group of hybrid delphiniums, the 'Pacific Giants', bred in California in the 1930s and 1940s, to satisfy Americans who longed to grow delphiniums. They grow up to 2.7m (9ft) tall and are well worth planting.

There are two scented species delphiniums that can be found in specialist nurseries. *D. brunonianum* is a native of the Himalayan foothills and makes a small plant just 20cm (8in) tall, so is ideal for growing in a rockery. It has flowers of the most delicate blue, with a black centre and purple-edged petals, which are strongly scented. *D. leroyi*, which grows in the middle of Africa, was reintroduced in the early 1960s and bears sweetly perfumed soft blue blooms. It is now being used in a breeding programme in Holland, to imbue modern varieties with its scent.

Delphiniums can be enjoyed in all their glory in the many gardens in Britain that open to the public. They are the backbone of a herbaceous border, so almost every garden of note grows them. Visiting a good garden is like a crash course in plantsmanship that can never be acquired from a book. Ideas can be taken home and mulled over during the long winter evenings, ready for action in summer.

FLOWERING SEASON: Summer, continuing to autumn.
SOIL CONDITIONS: Rich soil that drains freely.
SITUATE: Sun-loving, they need shelter from the wind because of their height.
PROPAGATION: Sow seed of species delphiniums at the beginning of spring. Hybrids don't come true from seed, so take base cuttings in late winter.
RESILIENCE: They can withstand some degree of frost.
CARE: Keep well watered and give a liquid feed once a fortnight. Tall examples need support. Dead-head them and the smaller shoots will flourish. Cut back when flowering is over. Watch out for common pests and diseases.

RIGHT: The stunning delphinium borders at Castle Howard in Yorkshire, England.

Dianthus (Caryophyllaceae)

pink

The exquisite pink has enjoyed a well-deserved popularity for centuries, for who could possibly resist its charm? Much hardier than carnations, their close relatives, pinks grow happily in the border, resulting in many survivors from yesteryear. Flowers grown in the seventeenth or eighteenth century are still being rediscovered in obscure gardens, where they have lived undisturbed for hundreds of years.

Although humble border plants, pinks have long been revered for their spicy scent. They were included in medieval posies that were carried to mask the odours of the day, and were thought to ward off the plague.

Pinks are native to central and southern Europe; the wild form is *Dianthus caryophyllus*. In Ancient Greece the sweetly scented flowers were woven into garlands and coronets. Theophrastus, a Greek philosopher of the fourth century BC, named them *diasanthos*, from the Greek words *dios*, meaning divine, and *anthos*, flower. The Swedish botanist Linnaeus, who was responsible for the binomial classification of plants, later shortened this to *Dianthus*.

It is thought that pinks first arrived in Britain at the time of the Norman Conquest, either deliberately imported by monks, or carried inadvertently as seeds adhering to the stones they brought with them to build their monasteries.

Pinks often formed part of medieval tithes: rents paid to the Lord of the Manor in either spring or autumn. Even if the tithe was of only one flower this was quite a task, because they are summer flowering. Their exquisite clove perfume made them an important ingredient in pot-pourri and perfumed sachets. One name, sop-in-wine, indicates their use as a flavouring for wine. They were among a selection of scented plants known as gillyflowers, a corruption of the French *girofle* or clove. (Wallflowers and stocks were also called gillyflowers.) They were depicted in manuscripts and Books of Hours, and embroidered into tapestries.

In the sixteenth century the English herbalist John Gerard noted that the pink 'endureth better the cold, and therefore is planted in gardens' – as opposed to the carnation, which was grown in pots and tended with care. He recorded the arrival from central Europe of the feathered pink (*D. plumarius*), which bears extraordinary ragged petals. This plant proved to be the basis for the pink's development.

In the late eighteenth century the laced pink emerged, having a distinct centre, with the colour repeated on the petals' edges. This first variety was called 'Lady Stoverdale'. It was developed by James Major, gardener to the Duchess of Lancaster, and caused great excitement. Muslin weavers in Lancashire and in Paisley, Scotland, and the coal miners of Northumberland, developed the variety further.

A great rivalry existed between the specialist pink societies of the north and the south of England. One celebrated variety was bred by the master of the workhouse in Slough and in 1880 was named 'Mrs Sinkins' after his wife. It had highly scented double, fringed white flowers, and was such a lasting sensation that it was incorporated into the borough of Slough's coat of arms. It is still enormously popular.

Enthusiasts classify pinks into four groups: selfs, which are all one colour; fancies with contrasting stripes and flecks; bi-colour, with a central eye and petals edged in a contrasting colour; and laced, which have a contrasting centre with each petal edged in the same colour.

FLOWERING SEASON: All summer long.

SOIL CONDITIONS: Neutral soil that drains freely.

SITUATE: In full sunshine.

PROPAGATION: Sow seed in early spring. Biennials can be sown directly in the garden in autumn or spring. In summer take cuttings from shoots that have not flowered.

RESILIENCE: Reliably hardy.

CARE: Water moderately if necessary in spring and on into summer. As usual, dead-head to prolong flowering. Watch out for aphids and slugs.

ABOVE AND LEFT: There is a great variety of forms within the genus *Dianthus*, from the extraordinary ragged petals of *D. chinensis* (left) to the furled and tightly packed petals of *D.* 'London Glow' (above).

Digitalis (Scrophulariaceae)

foxglove

Foxgloves are one of my favourite wildflowers. Natural inhabitants of woodland edges and lightly shaded clearings, they make ideal candidates for similar situations in today's garden. Equally, they look handsome standing to attention in anything from informal cottage beds to grand herbaceous displays.

Foxgloves grow in Central Asia, the northwest of Africa and all over Europe, and are steeped in fairy folklore. The flowers were supposed to be a gift to foxes from the fairies. Wearing them on its feet, a fox was able to sneak silently into poultry houses and wreak havoc. Foxgloves were best banned from the home because they were believed to encourage witches and the devil to enter. This belief was shared in most rural areas in the Middle Ages. Yet they were reputed to be the only plant with power to bring back children taken by the fairies and to identify changelings – children who had been substituted by the fairies. The symptoms of a changeling were a grumpy or whiny child, or one that suddenly became ill, so most children must have qualified at some point.

The foxglove, from the Old English foxes glofe, has many local names throughout the British Isles: fairy bells, granny's gloves, pop bells, ladies thimble and witches thimble, to name but a few. German botanist Leonard Fuchs (after whom the fuchsia was named) bestowed the Latin name *Digitali*s in 1542.

Foxgloves have long been used as a purgative against the 'king's evil' (scrofula or tuberculosis of the lymph glands) and dropsy. William Withering, an English physician, researched their properties and published his *Account of the Foxglove* in 1775. He proved that the plant acted on the heart, which led to further work in this field, culminating in the worldwide use of digitalis against heart disease to this day.

The native foxglove, *Digitalis purpurea*, was grown in gardens in the fifteenth century, and by the sixteenth century the white variety was

being planted and much admired. It was an essential component of the wilderness gardens of the eighteenth century.

There are about 20 species of *Digitalis*, both biennial and perennial. They are easily grown, making them a necessary if brief inclusion in any garden during early summer. The flowers range from white, yellow, pink and purple to golden brown, and are often spotted inside. Flowering in early summer, *D. lutea* is a joy in dappled shade, its pale yellow petals echoing the sunlight. This species, which is not too tall, has been grown with enthusiasm since the sixteenth century.

Brown is an intriguing flower colour and foxgloves can contribute a range of shades. The tall golden-brown to rusty-red spires of *D. ferruginea* look marvellous in mid-summer. Similarly eye-catching is the earlier flowering *D. parviflora*, which has dark orange-brown flowers.

These majestic plants are universally loved and children are enthralled by the accompanying tales of fairies and witches. If you conjure up this magic for your children, they can pass it on in turn to their families. In this way, ancient folklore survives.

ABOVE: *D. purpurea* grows happily at the edge of a wooded area.
LEFT: *D.* Excelsior Hybrid 'Sutton's Apricot'.
OPPOSITE: The speckled trumpets of *D.* 'Foxy Hybrid'.

FLOWERING SEASON: Late spring into summer.
SOIL CONDITIONS: They are tolerant, but added humus is a good idea.
SITUATE: In dappled shade.
PROPAGATION: If starting off in pots, sow in late spring. Sow in the garden where you wish them to be. Although many species are perennial, it is often easier to grow them as biennials.
RESILIENCE: Most are hardy, but some don't like frost.
CARE: Gloriously self-sufficient, but watch out for leafspot and powdery mildew.

Echinops (Asteraceae)
globe thistle

The globe thistle is aptly named. It produces dramatic drumstick-like flowerheads on stiff single stems that reach up to the sky. They come in shades of silvery white, grey and blue, and rise from a rosette of large, sculptural leaves. The deeply serrated foliage is beautiful too, and, being hairy escapes most garden pests. Silver and white are always useful colours in a garden, which is one of the reasons for the globe thistle's current popularity. Another is its sheer persistence – the plants go on and on, and even when the flowers are over their skeletal remains can be left for architectural interest in the winter border.

Its Latin name, *Echinops*, is taken from the Ancient Greek for sea-urchin, reflecting the spiky nature of the flowerheads before they open fully to reveal their long bugle-shaped blooms. The globe thistle is found on dry slopes and in grassland throughout India, Central Asia and central and southern Europe, which helps explain its undemanding nature in the garden. There are about 120 species, which include annuals, biennials and perennials.

Globe thistles spread throughout Europe in the sixteenth century, gradually becoming more popular, but it wasn't until the nineteenth century that their subtle beauty was universally recognised and they were included in many gardens. Today their place in a border is almost obligatory. *Echinops giganteus*, with soft, silvery blue blooms, lives up to its name and can reach 5m (15ft), with flowerheads up to 20cm (8in) across. It is ideal for adding interest to the back of a large border; it flowers in mid-summer and, if dead-headed, will produce a second flush. *E. sphaerocephalus* is a smaller plant (2.1m/7ft) with globes that are almost silver.

Globe thistles make excellent cut flowers, and also dry well for winter arrangements. The wild garden is an ideal site for these well-behaved plants. Their globes have a luminescent quality that is complemented by a sea of gently swaying meadow grass at their feet, while their misty understated colour enhances that of neighbouring plants.

FLOWERING SEASON: From mid-summer onwards.
SOIL CONDITIONS: They like poor soil that drains freely.
SITUATE: In sun or dappled shade.
PROPAGATION: The middle of spring is a good time to sow the seed in a prepared bed. Only seed from species will come true. Well-established clumps can be divided, both in spring and in autumn.
RESILIENCE: They are hardy and will withstand some degree of frost.
CARE: They are happily self-sufficient. Dead-head to stop self-seeding, unless you want great banks of them. Watch out for aphids.

LEFT: The dramatic flowerheads of *Echinops ritro* 'Veitch's Blue' in various stages of bloom.

Eryngium (Apiaceae)

sea holly

I know a windswept beach in northern Crete that is host to these charming plants. They grow in the barren sand, bringing to mind a line from Dylan Thomas, 'The force that through the green fuse drives the flower'. How can they thrive in such hostile conditions? The secret lies in their narrow leathery leaves that resist water loss and sun damage, and their deep roots.

Sea holly has had many uses through the centuries. In Ancient Greece it was known as erougerain, which means to deflate, because physicians of the period used the root of the plant to reduce swelling. In the sixteenth century it was a popular aphrodisiac and was grown in herb gardens for this purpose. At this time the herbalist John Gerard grew *Eryngium maritimum* and *E. planum*, which he described as the thistle of the sea and yringe.

New species arrived in Europe from North America at the end of the seventeenth century. The first to make an impact was *E. yuccifolium*, an evergreen perennial with sword-shaped leaves. During the mid-nineteenth century *E. agavifolium* arrived from the Argentine. These are both tall varieties, with quite different foliage from their European counterparts.

Eryngiums are versatile plants that self-seed and naturalise with ease. *E. giganteum* is better known by its common name Miss Willmott's ghost, after the famous Edwardian gardener who made it her calling card. She sprinkled seeds around when she visited gardens and, being biennial, two years later the plants flowered, seemingly from nowhere.

Some species make good container plants. Drought-tolerant, sun-loving *E. x tripartitum* bears flowers of a deep blue, almost purple, and *E. proteiflorum*, from Mexico, produces shimmering flowers of a softer blue.

FLOWERING SEASON: From the middle of summer to the onset of winter.
SOIL CONDITIONS: They enjoy poor soil but it must be freely draining.
SITUATE: In full sun.
PROPAGATION: Sow ripe seed in pots in a coldframe. Divide established clumps in spring.
RESILIENCE: They are mostly hardy but some varieties are susceptible to frost.
CARE: They do not like to get wet, so protect them in winter. Watch out for slugs and powdery mildew.

LEFT: The contrast between the forms of eryngium and bellflowers is even more startling because of their similarity in colour.
OPPOSITE: Close-up, the spiky bracts have an almost sinister quality.

ABOVE: The rich orange tones of *Erysimum cheiri* 'Orange Bedder'.

Erysimum (Brassicaceae)

wallflower

In spring the rich velvety hues of wallflowers are hugely welcome. Colour returns to the garden, buds pop open, leaves shake themselves free and the whole garden is preparing for the glories to come. The much-loved wallflower is one of the flowers that mark the end of winter.

The old botanical name *Cheiranthus* means handflower in Greek, conferred because the wallflower was an essential ingredient in medieval nosegays. Its common name reflects its habit of growing happily in the crevices of old stone walls.

Wallflowers hail from southern Europe and the Aegean. The Romans may have introduced them to the British Isles, but the most beguiling tale is that the seeds arrived at the time of the Norman conquest along with the pink (see page 58), clinging to stones brought from France to build castles and abbeys. The plants are now naturalised in some places.

Elizabethan gardeners called wallflowers by the Old English word for comfort, *chevisaunce*, which sounds delightful to modern ears. This was partly because of their scent, but also because the plants are long-lived, so they were seen as symbols of faithfulness. Along with the stock and sweet-rocket, Elizabethans also called

them gillyflowers from the French *girofle*, meaning clove and referring to their scent. By the sixteenth century the herbalist John Gerard, was calling them yellow stock-gillyflowers. Another herbalist of the period, John Parkinson, alluded to them as wall-gilloflowers and described seven types, which included doubles of yellow and of red. One of these – a bushy double yellow, deeply scented plant – was illustrated in his book *Paradisus in sole paradisus terrestris* of 1629. Wallflowers were taken to America with the first settlers, and swiftly became established there.

By Georgian and Victorian times wallflowers had become fashionable garden plants, particularly the doubles. Nowadays double forms of the old varieties of wallflowers have all but vanished.

However, in the late nineteenth century a Reverend Harpur-Crewe rescued a small bushy example identical to the one illustrated in Parkinson's *Paradisus*. He gave cuttings to his friends, who called it 'Harpur Crewe', the name it is still known by today.

Wallflowers are easy to cultivate and have always been stalwarts of the cottage garden. The soft warm colours of their flowers and their small size make them ideal for a late-spring border – they provide a perfect foil for tulips. For example, the deepest velvety wallflowers, such as the smaller 'Blood Red', mix well with *Tulipa* 'Queen of the Night', which has flowers of deepest damson. A bed of bronze wallflowers is particularly eye-catching in the soft light of spring, but I also love deep dark rich reds.

Today the wallflower is a prominent component of municipal planting. Roundabouts positively glow with them and to stroll through some of the great city parks in spring is a treat. These well-tended spaces are invaluable in cities, offering a much-needed respite from the hurried life we all seem to lead nowadays.

FLOWERING SEASON: Spring and on into summer if dead-headed.
SOIL CONDITIONS: Poor soil that drains freely.
SITUATE: In full sun, but in a sheltered position.
PROPAGATION: Sow seed in summer for bedding plants, the following spring for flowers. Take cuttings of perennials in summer and overwinter in a coldframe.
RESILIENCE: Hardy.
CARE: Vulnerable to various fungal diseases and plant viruses. Watch out for slugs and snails.

Euphorbia (Euphorbiaceae)

spurge

It is always exhilarating to find plants usually associated with the garden border, in their natural environment. Euphorbias grow abundantly on the lower slopes of the craggy mountains of Crete. Their muted graduated colours soften the harsh landscape, transforming it into a wonderful natural rock garden that could never be reproduced artificially.

Euphorbia is a hugely diverse genus that encompasses the poinsettia castor-oil plant and great succulent trees that grow in South Africa. But the euphorbias that are native to the Mediterranean and are grown with great success in gardens worldwide are the spurges. The plants are named after Euphorbus, a physician in Ancient Greece, and their common name is derived from the Latin *expurgare*, meaning to purge – reflecting their medicinal use.

Another Greek physician, Dioscorides, gives many uses for the plant in his herbal of the first century AD. The milky sap was used as a purgative, emetic and diuretic, and to cure warts, but it is also a poisonous irritant and stimulant.

For centuries euphorbias were usually grown in physick gardens. It was certainly known to the Tradescants, the renowned seventeenth-century English gardeners, who included it in their plant lists of 1629. Then in the nineteenthcentury Gertrude Jekyll championed *Euphorbia characias* ssp. *wulfenii* as a garden ornamental and eurhorbias took off with a vengeance. *E. characias* is still fashionable.

A sport of *E. characias* called 'Lamberhurst Gold' is being nurtured with some secrecy, and

OPPOSITE: The green 'flowers' of *Euphorbia characias* are actually bracts surrounding the insignificant-look-

softest lemon-yellow and white will burst upon the scene, no doubt to enormous excitement.

In the interim there are many excellent varieties that can be grown with ease. It is not difficult to reproduce the dry natural gardens of the Mediterranean in northern temperate zones and, as global warming seems to be taking effect, plants that thrive in arid conditions are more than welcome.

Spurges are invaluable in a garden, for they impart structure and form and make wonderful building blocks for the border. In one garden I have seen great banks of *E. characias* planted each side of a drive. Since they have a tendency to become leggy, they are underplanted with the smaller *E. amygdaloides* var. *robbiae* at their feet. The result is a year-round display, changing colour with the seasons. In early summer it forms a stylish contrast with the stunning iris walks alongside.

E. palustris from Europe is a good garden plant, bearing great yellow heads of bracts that last well into autumn. There are many species to choose from. Browse through a specialist catalogue and you'll be sure to find plants that will complement your garden.

FLOWERING SEASON: From the beginning of spring to the onset of summer.
SOIL CONDITIONS: Well-drained rich soil.
SITUATE: In sun-dappled shade, according to species.
PROPAGATION: Sow seed of annuals direct in the garden. Sow perennials in pots under glass in spring. Divide established clumps of perennials in early spring or take cuttings from the base.
RESILIENCE: They are hardy, but can be susceptible to frost.
CARE: Generally self-sufficient, but watch out for aphids. Do not plant close to garden ponds as the sap is poisonous to fish.

RIGHT: The drooping bracts of *Euphorbia characias* make it an unusual feature in a garden border.
OPPOSITE: *Euphorbia amygdaloides* has red crescent-shaped centres that contrast strikingly with its pale green bracts.

Freesia (Iridaceae)

freesia

In Australia I saw a lake surrounded by bluebells and white freesias – a breathtaking sight. The delicate flowers swayed in the early morning breeze, releasing their heady perfume. They had been planted with great care and appeared to be as natural as any bluebell wood. Blue and white is a classic colour combination, the white making the blue appear even more intense. It was a stunning composition to behold on such a vast scale.

Freesias are actually natives of the Cape region of South Africa. They were first recorded as being cultivated in Europe in 1786 by Dr Friedreich Heinrich Theodor Freese, a physician in Kiel, Germany who gave the plants their name. Yet they didn't become truly popular until the late nineteenth century and early twentieth century. There are perhaps six species, but today there are more than 300 cultivars, grown mostly for the cut-flower trade and prized for their exquisite perfume – rare in flowers from South Africa. White freesias are the most strongly scented, in common with most white flowers. With the development of coloured varieties of any scented species, the perfume diminishes.

Freesias grow from corms that send up usually one flower stem. They are not very hardy but can be grown outside in areas that are not too frost-prone, where they flower elegantly in spring, their waxy fragrant flowers held above knife-like tapering foliage. If your garden is not sheltered enough, they make good greenhouse and house plants. Sunny windowsills are their ideal habitat and, once in flower, their delicious scent fills the house for several weeks. The freesia is one of the most popular cut flowers, its pure simplicity refreshing as it sweetens the air.

FLOWERING SEASON: From the end of spring through to summer.
SOIL CONDITIONS: Fairly rich soil that drains freely.
SITUATE: Shade from the sun while young if under glass. Outdoors they thrive on sunlight.
PROPAGATION: Sow seed at the end of the year under glass. In areas with rare frost the corms may be planted in autumn. In areas susceptible to frost they can be planted in spring. Detach offsets when corms are lifted.
RESILIENCE: They are only half-hardy and do not like frost.
CARE: Under glass they need feeding with a liquid fertiliser, but they are self-sufficient in the garden. Beware aphids. In cold areas lift corms in autumn and overwinter in a frost-free shed.

OPPOSITE: The snow-white blooms of *Freesia lactea* are more strongly scented than many of the coloured varieties.

fritillary

There are about 100 species of fritillaries growing in the temperate northern hemisphere. Probably the most familiar in British gardens are the snake's head fritillaries, with their extraordinary chequered petals of purple (and sometimes white). They also grow wild in low-lying water meadows, though whether they are the native species or naturalised garden escapes is a matter of botanical debate. The main argument centres on the fact that they were not recorded as growing in the wild until 1736, whereas John Gerard, the sixteenth-century herbalist, grew them in his garden. He wrote of the fritillary as resembling 'the table or board upon which men plaie at chesse'. He called it the 'checquered dafodill' and also the 'ginny-hen floure'. This name was inspired by the snake's head fritillary's chequered petals, which look like a guinea-fowl's feathers. The same association is made in the Latin name, *Fritillaria meleagris*: *meleagris* means guinea-fowl; *fritillaria* is from *fritillus*, a dice box, which refers to the flower's shape. Gerard also noted that they are 'greatly esteemed for the beautifying of our gardens and bosoms of the beautiful'. The fritillaries that survive in meadows today may sometimes be the progeny of the long-disappeared grounds of large country houses. Some protected sites may well have remained undisturbed since the time of the Tudors.

Another familiar garden fritillary is the crown imperial, *F. imperialis*, native of the Western Himalayas, southern Russia, Turkey and Iran. Also known as the Persian lily, it was cultivated by the Turks and introduced to Vienna in the late sixteenth century, and from there to England. In his *Herball* of 1597, Gerard states that 'the plant likewise hath been brought from Constantinople, amongst other bulbous roots, and made denizens in our London gardens where I have great plenty'. He must have had the most well-stocked garden of all time. One of the crown imperial's other names is tears of Mary.

Legend has it that, being full of pride, the flower did not bow its head when Christ entered the Garden of Gethsemane. Because of this it has blushed, drooped its head and cried in penitence ever since. The 'tears' are the ever-present drops of nectar in its flowers.

The crown imperial has been grown in cottage gardens for countless years. My mother, who grew up in rural Suffolk during Queen Victoria's reign, used to tell of their importance in the May Queen's crown, for no crown was complete without one.

The black sarana, *F. camschatcensis*, is a strikingly different fritillary. It is a native of western North America, reaching as far north as Alaska, and also growing in Asia in north-eastern regions. Its sweet-smelling blooms are almost black in hue, hence its common name. Another virtually black-flowered example is *F. persica*, which bears numerous bells of a wonderful dark brownish purple.

For the non-specialist gardener the snake's head fritillary is easily established in grass or meadow gardens, or in beds if given a soil with added humus, for it likes to have damp feet. The crown imperial is more difficult and must be planted deeply if it is to thrive – up to 45cm (18in). Even so it may flower one year but not the next; an annual winter top-dressing of manure can help. The soil also needs to be free-draining. Research has indicated that crown imperials may be pollinated by small birds trying to get at their nectar, which is not so preposterous as it sounds because there is an American fritillary already known to be pollinated by humming birds.

It is also worth trying to grow the more capricious species of fritillaries, because even a small success helps protect them for the future. Some can be introduced into wildflower meads with ease; some can be grown as alpines in a rock garden, where their delicacy complements the other flowers of spring.

FLOWERING SEASON: They are spring flowering and last until the onset of summer.
SOIL CONDITIONS: Rich soil that drains freely.
SITUATE: Some enjoy sunshine, some dappled shade.
PROPAGATION: Sow seed in a coldframe in autumn. This requires patience it is very slow to germinate.
RESILIENCE: Hardy.
CARE: Don't let bulbs dry out, but make sure they don't become waterlogged. Watch out for slugs and lily beetle.

ABOVE: Crown imperials need to be planted deeply if they are to flower as spectacularly as these specimens.
BELOW: The familiar snake's head fritillary (*Fritillaria meleagris*), often found growing wild.
OPPOSITE: The stately *Fritillaria imperialis* 'Lutea', commonly known as crown imperial.

Geranium (Geraniaceae) hardy geranium

cranesbill

The abundant foliage that blankets the ground under the delicate cups of the hardy geranium is almost as beautiful as its flowers. Like a soft carpet of pale green velvet, it provides a colour-wash, masking the ground beneath and acting as a foil for other members of the border. The first geranium I ever grew was *Geranium clarkei* 'Kashmir White', whose delicately veined white petals glow in the soft twilight. Thus began my love affair with these plants.

The geranium or cranesbill should not be confused with the pelargonium, a native of South Africa that is erroneously called a geranium and grown as a pot plant and for bedding displays. There are about 300 species in the true genus *Geranium*, both annual and perennial, and there are also some semi-evergreen varieties. They are characterised by their seedpods, which have a beak-like point, hence the name geranium from *geranos*, Ancient Greek for crane and a reference to the bird's beak.

Native wild plants have been cultivated in English gardens since early times. Then European varieties began to arrive, and by the late sixteenth century Gerard, the renowned herbalist, recorded them as growing in his garden, particularly *G. phaeum*, the dusky cranesbill or mourning widow, which has since become naturalised. He also advocated their medicinal properties: the powdered roots in a decoction of wine were thought to be beneficial for internal disorders.

Geraniums are found throughout dry temperate regions and bear cup-like flowers of white, pink, purple and blue. The plants are generally amenable to grow and are long-lived.

They will tolerate almost any conditions: hot dry slopes, damp shade and – the bane of every gardener – dry shade. They are invaluable as ground cover, as the plants form clumps that merge into each other. They flower from late spring to late summer, with many delicate blooms being borne on each plant.

G. macrorrhizum is a ground-cover species that has masses of pink flowers in spring and agreeably aromatic foliage that turns deep red after frost. It positively flourishes in dry shade and self-seeds readily.

I have grown geraniums very successfully in pots and butler's sinks in the garden. Surviving severe neglect and long absences, each spring the soft shoots unfurl, and I wait for the delicate flowers to emerge. They provide pleasure above and beyond the call of duty, and remain much-loved permanent residents in my small patch.

FLOWERING SEASON: From late spring through to autumn.
SOIL CONDITIONS: Very tolerant.
SITUATE: Equally happy in sunlight or dappled shade.
PROPAGATION: Divide clumps in spring or early summer. Species will come true from seed and may self-seed.
RESILIENCE: Some species are hardy, some frost prone.
CARE: Remove flowers and leaves as they wither, so that more will follow. Watch out for slugs, snails and mildew.

ABOVE LEFT: *Geranium* 'Claridge Druce', whose magenta flowers will add a dash of colour to any area of the garden.
RIGHT: *G. pratense* is commonly known as the meadow cranesbill. This one is 'Mrs Kendall Clarke'.
OVERLEAF: *G.* 'Versicolor' has a delicate tracery of colour on its petals.

Gladiolus (Iridaceae)

gladiolus

The sight of wild gladioli in bloom in the olive groves of Crete in spring is a feast for the eyes. Villagers call the plants knives and, indeed, the Latin name derives from *gladius*, a sword or spear. In the village where I often stay my neighbours nod with approval as I bring them to the house, so presumably they have no superstition attached to them. Over the centuries, man has changed the gladiolus but, to me, has not been able to improve on its wild form.

There were once wild gladioli in profusion in Britain, too. The now very rare wild gladiolus of Britain is *Gladiolus illyricus*, its common name being corn flag. These plants were grown in borders in the sixteenth and seventeenth centuries. The sixteenth-century herbalist John Gerard recommended the corn flagge for garnishing and decking London gardens.

He was also familiar with the gladioli of Ancient Greece: *G. communis*, *G. communis* ssp. *byzantinus* and *G. segetum*. The latter grows in abundance in the olive groves and cornfields of southern Europe, and is particularly prolific in Crete. Some say it can claim to be the Huakinthos or Hyacinthus of Greek mythology, as its petals bear markings that can be deciphered as AI-AI, the Ancient Greek cry of woe. Hyacinthus, beloved of Apollo, was slain by him in error and the plant was dedicated to Hyacinthus. The gladiolus may also have adorned the boys who celebrated the festival of the goddess Demeter, as it grows in cornfields.

Dioscorides, writing in the first century AD, recommended the upper corm as an aphrodisiac. Theophrastus suggested cooking the corm and adding it to bread flour to sweeten it; apparently the flavour is not unlike that of chestnuts.

The gladiolus grown with such enthusiasm today comes from Africa (particularly South Africa), and was imported to Europe at the end of the eighteenth century. The first scented species to arrive was the delicately pallid *G. tristis*, which smells sweetest at night. It is a native

of Natal and was being grown in the Chelsea Physick Garden by the mid-eighteenth century.

Gladioli soon became enormously popular as exhibition flowers, and nurserymen developed and introduced thousands of hybrids and cultivars. Today there are some 10,000 varieties available. As is often the case with highly developed varieties, colour and shape are maximised at the expense of attributes such as scent. But work is currently underway in this area to produce a perfumed strain hardy enough for northern climates.

In the garden gladioli look handsome planted in clumps, their knife-like leaves and shafts of flowers adding a welcome vertical dimension, and there is certainly a choice of colour to suit every scheme. Planted among flowers of softer foliage of a complementary colour, they are very eye-catching. Species gladioli tend to be daintier and easier to use in a mixed border. After all, varieties bred as exhibition flowers were never intended to take their place in a border, but rather to stand out among their peers and catch the judge's eye at flower shows. The great spears of flowers look as wonderful in the home as at flower shows, however, lighting up dark corners and hallways.

FLOWERING SEASON: From the end of spring until summer draws to a close.

SOIL CONDITIONS: Rich free-draining soil is to their liking.

SITUATE: In sunshine.

PROPAGATION: Seed can be sown in pots under glass in spring, but it's easier to separate offsets from the corms when you lift them in autumn, and grow these on in pots.

RESILIENCE: Mostly frost-tender.

CARE: They benefit from a liquid fertiliser once a fortnight. Lift the corms after the plants have faded and store in a cool frost-free shed. Watch out for slugs, aphids and botrytis.

RIGHT AND OPPOSITE: Gladioli can be grown with great success as cutting flowers, and they are staples of modern florists.

Gunnera (Gunneraceae) giant ornamental rhubarb

gunnera

The gunnera is one of nature's sublime achievements. It is impossible to walk by this plant without being overwhelmed by its scale and rugged beauty, for it is a magnificent sight. The rhubarb-like leaves can reach up to 3m (10ft) tall, with each leaf spanning an impressive 2m (7ft). And the plant's aggressively prickly stems and prehistoric-looking flower spikes produced each summer help reinforce its dramatic presence. If that were not enough, this giant of a plant is herbaceous, so thrusts up its huge canopy from scratch in a matter of weeks each spring.

The gunnera, named after the eminent eighteenth-century Norwegian Bishop Ernst Gunnerus, who was also a botanist, is native to the damp boggy areas of South America, Australia, Asia and South Africa.

In 1873 a description and portrait of *Gunnera brephogea* was published in *L'Illustration Horticole*, a French horticultural magazine. It had been discovered by chance. An epiphytic orchid was sent from Grenada and its roots were attached to the gunnera, which subsequently proved just as interesting – if not more so – than the orchid.

Simultaneously another species, this time from Brazil, was discovered, namely *G. manicata*, a hugely impressive plant that ensured the species was sent around the world. The rootstock was widely distributed to plant lovers, became a popular specimen plant, and has remained so ever since.

G. manicata is one of the largest-leaved plants on earth. The hackneyed words sculptural and architectural are simply inadequate to describe this giant. The enormous deeply incised leaves, like great umbrellas, are born on towering stems. They cast great dark reflections on the water they love to grow beside, evoking a sense of mystery and – in a temperate garden – of the gloriously exotic. These shapely leaves shield tall panicles of tiny flowers, which range from amber to bronze-tinged green in early summer, and are followed by round amber-to-green fruit.

Few people have a lake, bog-garden or even a pond large enough to accommodate these spectacular giants, but thanks to some of the many private gardens now open to the public, it is possible for all to enjoy and marvel at their curiosity. However, you can grow a single specimen in a half-barrel filled with a moisture-retaining compost. Whether you grow gunnera in pots or in the garden, in frost-prone areas protect crowns of plants when the leaves die back. One method is to pile the dying leaves on top of the crown to help insulate it. You might want to add straw or horticultural fleece for extra protection.

FLOWERING SEASON: Summer flowering.
SOIL CONDITIONS: Moist soil that contains humus.
SITUATE: In sunshine or dappled shade.
PROPAGATION: They are difficult to grow from seed. Basal buds can be taken as cuttings in spring, and grown on in pots protected from frost.
RESILIENCE: Not fully hardy – frost-prone.
CARE: Shelter the larger species from cold winds. In areas prone to frost it is a good idea to dry-mulch the crowns as a protection. Watch out for slugs.

LEFT AND RIGHT: It is easy to see how *Gunnera manicata*, shown here growing in private gardens, acquired its common name of giant ornamental rhubarb, but despite its size the unfurling leaves have a touch of delicacy about them.

Helianthus annuus (Asteraceae)

sunflower

The great golden discs of the annual sunflower embody all that is summer, as their great flowerheads turn to follow their namesake through the heavens. The sunflower is one of the most popular garden flowers. In colour it spans the whole range of browns and yellows, from the deep bronze of the variety 'Floristan' to the almost citric lemon of 'Vanilla Ice' with its dark chocolate centre. Every one is guaranteed to look spectacular in a garden, whether to brighten up a dull corner, provide a splash of gold at the back of a herbaceous border or create a seasonal focal point. Even when flowers fade, the dried seedheads provide structure and colour for all manner of arrangements indoors, and can look extremely good if simply left in the garden.

The sunflower gets its name because the flower follows the sun's path across the sky each day. It's a straight translation of the Latin name, which comes from the Greek *helios*, meaning sun, and *anthos*, flower. According to legend, Helios, the Greek god of the sun, was drowned by his uncles, the Titans, and has resided in the sky ever since.

The annual sunflower, *Helianthus annuus*, is one of 70 or so species that include some perennials, too. It was first admired by the Incan civilisation in Peru. To the Incas it represented the sun god, and its image has been found carved on their temples. When writing of discoveries in the New World, Nicholas Monardes, a plant collector of the sixteenth century, summed up the sunflower as follows: 'a strange flower, for it casteth out the greatest flowers, and the most particulars that ever hath been seen, for it is greater than a great platter or dish, the which have diverse colours, it showeth marvellous fair in the gardines.'

At this time many newly collected plants went to the garden at Blois in France, which was owned by Gaston, Duc d' Orleans, the brother of Louis XIII. From the work of botanical artists we know that the sunflower was an early resident. In England it has been grown since Elizabethan times and was one of the plants written about by the herbalist John Gerard, who evoked the seedheads as 'much like the honeycomb of bees'. Sunflowers were also prized by the Victorians. Their impressive 'bouquet' gardens, which displayed prized plants of that era, featured sunflowers. To copy this idea today, use the sunflower as a glorious focal point. By combining both tall and small varieties and surrounding them with other yellow and bronze flowers, such as helenium, rudbeckia, crocosmia, and perhaps at the base golden oregano and a tumble of nasturtiums, you can create a hot display that will warm the heart.

Sunflowers have always intrigued scientists, not only for their ability to follow the sun's rays, but also because they are one of the most perfect examples of the link between mathematics and nature. The way in which the leaves grow on the stem forms a perfect spiral from base to top in an exact measured mathematical progression. This formation was identified in the twelfth century by the Italian mathematician Leonardo Fibonacci, who gave his name to the Fibonacci series, where each number in the series equals the sum of the two preceding numbers.

The seeds of the sunflower have been used in a variety of ways over the centuries. They are a delicious source of food: roasted, they can be eaten on their own, mixed in with bread dough and baked, or even sprouted for salads. The seeds are also crushed for oil.

Varieties of annual sunflower grow successfully in most climates. Kansas, in the USA (where it is a native of the great plains), has adopted it as its state flower. In France, especially in the south, visitors can be overwhelmed by vast acres of the flowers. Standing in serried ranks, they hold their heads high as they follow the sun, only to bow them in sorrow at dusk until they are awoken once more by the dawn.

FLOWERING SEASON: From the middle to the end of summer.
SOIL CONDITIONS: Rich soil with added humus that drains freely.
SITUATE: In full sunshine, as their name suggests.
PROPAGATION: Annuals can be sown in the garden in both spring and autumn.
RESILIENCE: Annuals are hardy.
CARE: A long hot summer is necessary to get a really good display. Tall species need to be supported.

OPPOSITE: The huge flowerheads of *Helianthus annuus* 'Gold Spot' are a magnet for butterflies and bees.

Heliconia (Musaceae)

wild plantain

Heliconias kindle a feeling of disbelief on first acquaintance. Towering above mere mortals, they are indeed fantastic and one is filled with awe in their presence. Related to the more familiar bird of paradise flower (see Strelitzia, page 168), they produce tall exotic leaves shaped like paddles, from which their dramatic blooms emerge. The claw-like bracts that enclose the flowers come in the brightest of reds, yellows and oranges and they look rather like lobster claws. These tropical beauties have become extremely popular with flower arrangers, which is understandable, for they are very long-lasting as cut flowers and are readily available from florists worldwide.

The extraordinary heliconia family is named after Mount Helicon, home of the Muses of Greek myth. It is a native of tropical America, and some Pacific islands. In Australia I met a dedicated couple who garden in the tropical rainforest of northern Queensland. Helen and John Richardson have worked tirelessly in their private botanical garden, Bellenden-Kerr, for the past 25 years. To help fund their conservation work with rainforest species they have built up a thriving cut-flower business by importing heliconias and growing them for the floristry trade. Each day they send shipments of these exotic beauties from nearby Cairns to the flower shops of Sydney. They saw the plant's potential at once, though some florists took a little more time to be convinced of their beauty.

Walking through the surrounding rainforest, home to untold poisonous creatures such as tree pythons and deadly spiders, was a truly extraordinary experience. Encountering a lavender python is etched for ever on my memory. Fortunately the Richardsons are unperturbed by such things, and so we are able to enjoy their flowers in the comfort of our homes. Devoted conservationists are essential to the continued existence of the rainforest. It is being destroyed at such a pace that countless species will disappear, unless people are prepared to dedicate their time and energy to its preservation.

FLOWERING SEASON: All year long.

SOIL CONDITIONS: Outdoors grow in freely draining humus-rich soil. Indoors grow in a half-and-half mixture of pulverised bark and peat.

SITUATE: In dappled shade, sheltered from the wind.

PROPAGATION: Sow seed in spring. Divide the rhizomes of established clumps in spring.

RESILIENCE: They are susceptible to frost.

CARE: Grown indoors, they must be kept moist during the growing season and benefit from a dose of liquid fertiliser every four weeks. Outdoors they enjoy the moist humid conditions of the rainforest.

LEFT AND OPPOSITE: The amazing flowers of heliconia hardly look like flowers at all, and have an exotic beauty unlike any other flower.

Helleborus (Ranunculaceae)

hellebore

Walking through the mountains of northern Greece once, I was astonished to come across meadows full of hellebores. Being used to seeing them planted with care in a garden setting, to see them *en masse* was incredible. I shouldn't have been surprised, because Greece has the most abundant wildflower population in all Europe. This is in part thanks to the difficult terrain, but more significant perhaps, is the inhabitants' unwillingness to poison their environment with chemicals.

Hellebores possess fearsome medicinal properties; they are deadly poisonous and have always been used with caution. According to myth, Melampes, the physician and soothsayer of legend, used the Christmas rose (*Helleborus niger*) as a purgative and cure for the melancholia of the daughters of Proteus, King of Argos in

about 1500 BC. The physician Dioscorides recommended it for 'driving out phelgm and choler'; he went on to say 'it is good for ye epilepticall, melancholicall, frantick, arthriticall and paraliticall, but given in a pessum it expels ye menstrua and kills ye embrya'. The Roman scholar Pliny the Elder, writing in the first century AD, warned of its poisonous nature: 'the black hellebore is a very poison to horses, kine and oxen'. Yet horse doctors in the sixteenth century found a use for the native European *H. viridis*. It was taken to New England with the first American settlers, where it became naturalised.

Seventeenth-century English housewives grew hellebores for use against boils and also worms in children – dangerous as it was possible to kill both the worms and the child. Herbalist John Gerard advised that the hellebore was best used by 'country people which feed grossely and have hard, rough and strong bodies'.

H. foetidus, a native of Europe and Asia, with bright green bunches of flowers was popular with late-seventeenth-century gardeners and is enjoying a renaissance today. *H. lividus* and *H. corsicus* (now known as *H. argutifolius*), from the islands of the Mediterranean, were introduced to Britain in the mid-nineteenth century. *H. orientalis* from Greece and Turkey was also thought to have reached these shores around this time. *Edwards Botanical Register* of 1842 describes it as 'vastly rare'. Half a century later Gertrude Jekyll's use of them in her garden at Munstead Wood excited great interest and they have gained in favour ever since.

The plants, with their deeply serrated long lasting leaves and flowers, which range from white-green through pink to black, are now enjoying a huge revival. Their flowering season from winter through to spring brings shape and interest when gardens are otherwise bare, and their subtle colours light up gloomy corners and borders. They also make superb cut flowers seemingly subtle but on closer inspection intricately marked and remarkably beautiful. Annoyingly for gardeners, snails seem to be impervious to the plants' poisonous defences but in return they spread the seeds of the plant in their slime.

To tend plants that have been grown since ancient times makes one feel slightly insignificant. Modern breeders are producing exciting new varieties, with blue-black and yellow forms now being developed. So these ancient plants survive and their future looks assured.

FLOWERING SEASON: Early winter until late spring.
SOIL CONDITIONS: They are accommodating but like damp rich soil and benefit from added humus.
SITUATE: Shelter them in dappled shade.
PROPAGATION: Sow seeds when ripe in a coldframe. After flowering, established clumps can be divided.
RESILIENCE: They are hardy but can be frost-prone.
CARE: Keep them moist with plenty of humus when planting. Watch out for snails, slugs and aphids. Remove last year's leaves to show off flowers.

ABOVE LEFT: All-green sprays of *Helleborus foetidus* provide a textural focus in a border.
RIGHT: The delicate blooms of the Christmas rose (*H. niger*).
OVERLEAF: *H. x hybridus* 'Peggy Ballard'

day lily

Hemerocallis (Hemerocallidaceae)

The beautiful day lilies are, for me, at their most attractive where they have escaped to the wild. Popular garden plants in North America during colonial times, they have since naturalised and great swathes of them grow on the margins of woods, in meadows and on roadsides. I always associate them with one particular route: as I drove along the Massachusetts Turnpike that carves its way through the wilderness, their sparkling orange flowers seemed to glow against the dark foliage like golden stars.

Although each flower lasts for but a day, new flowers open in succession to give a continuous display from early to mid-summer. And since some varieties are later blooming, an extended season of colour is possible. Their strap-like semi-evergreen foliage is pleasing in the border all year round.

As with the common name, the Latin one reflects the fleeting beauty of the flowers. It comes from the Greek words *hemera*, meaning day, and *kallos*, beauty. Hemerocallis has been cultivated since ancient times. It was grown in China thousands of years ago for its flowers and for its culinary and medicinal uses. The flowers were eaten dried or salted, and the buds, known as *gum tsoy*, or golden vegetables, are considered a great delicacy. The young leaves are said to be intoxicating: the Chinese call the day lily *hsuan t'sao*, the plant of forgetfulness, and used it as a cure for sorrow.

The highly lemon-scented *Hemerocallis flava* (now renamed *H. lilioasphodelus*) was known by the Egyptians and Romans and recorded by Dioscorides, a physician of Ancient Greece.

Reaching England in the mid-fifteenth century, this was probably the variety grown by herbalist John Gerard in his garden in London. He said that they were grown by 'herbarists, and lovers of fine and rare plants'. He also recommended them as a cure for 'hot swelling in the dugges' after childbirth 'and likewise taketh away the inflamation of the eys'.

The Swedish botanist Linnaeus believed that the unscented orange *H. fulva* originated in China and speculated that it reached the West along the silk routes. A double form of *H. fulva* was introduced to Europe from Japan in the mid-nineteenth century and became very popular. The end of the century saw many new species arriving in Europe, but many more were exported to North America directly from Japan and were then re-exported to Europe.

Day lilies thrived in the climatic conditions of America and, although the very first ventures in breeding started in Europe – Amos Perry producing wonderful examples in the early twentieth century – American enthusiasts produced even more spectacular varieties and continue to do so. Day lilies are also bred enthusiastically in Australia where they are highly prized. The result of this labour is about 30,000 choices, in colours ranging from nearly white, through yellow, orange, scarlet and dark purple to an almost black variety.

The plants naturalise happily in woodland. The dwarf varieties are ideal for smaller gardens and grow well in containers, but great drifts of the sweetly scented *H. flava* in a wild garden are hard to surpass.

ABOVE: As their name suggests, the flowers only last for one day, so a decent-sized area of the garden needs to be given over to day lilies to ensure colour for the longest possible period.
OPPOSITE: *Hemerocallis* 'Ruffled Apricot'.

FLOWERING SEASON: From the onset of summer to the middle.
SOIL CONDITIONS: Rich damp soil.
SITUATE: In full sunshine.
PROPAGATION: Seed can be sown in pots under glass in both spring and autumn. Established clumps can be divided both in spring and autumn – evergreens in spring only.
RESILIENCE: Usefully hardy.
CARE: They benefit from a mulch in both spring and autumn. Keep moist and apply a liquid fertiliser every two weeks until the flowerbuds are established. Watch out for aphids, thrips and rust.

Heracleum (Umbelliferae)

giant hogweed

To come upon the giant hogweed unexpectedly is like encountering something from outer space. The vast umbrellas of its flowers are held on great thick towering stems taller than a man. My first encounter with this titan of the plant world was in a friend's garden. The plant was like something from Alice in Wonderland and we seemed insignificant beside it.

Heracleum mantegazzianum, a giant of a plant, is aptly named after Hercules and is a native of Eurasia and North America. It gets its common name from its smaller European relative *H. sphondylium*, which grows in hedgerows and on roadsides. This European native has long been grubbed up and eaten by pigs and is commonly known as hogweed.

Giant hogweed was established as an ornamental garden plant in Britain by 1835. It is ideal to plant as an impressive specimen and a novelty, but it has an extremely invasive nature as it self-seeds like wildfire. In 1870 William Robinson recommended them as good plants for 'rough places on the banks of rivers', but cautioned that they should not be allowed to self seed and 'become giant weeds'. As he predicted, garden escapees can colonise areas very rapidly and smother native plants, leading to the Wildlife and Countryside Act of 1981 declaring it an offence to plant this great architectural treasure in the wild or to cause it to grow there. Yet it still grows in great banks beside busy suburban main roads, the wind spreading the seeds, and, as this is urban wasteland, it survives.

The plant should be treated with respect in the garden or the wild. Its sap contains photochemical irritants that make the skin hypersensitive to light and so cause painful burn-like weals. I have grown giant hogweed and even cut and dried it for the house. I was careful to wear gloves and suffered no ill effects.

Provided you bear these points in mind, it still makes a stunning specimen plant, perhaps hidden from view so as to be chanced upon on a stroll, and its mysterious and slightly sinister quality be all the more appreciated.

FLOWERING SEASON: Mid-summer.
SOIL CONDITIONS: Poor to moderately rich soil that drains freely.
SITUATE: In dappled woodland conditions.
PROPAGATION: Just scatter the pungent seed.
RESILIENCE: Hardy and resilient. Weedkiller has little or no effect on it.
CARE: Remove seedheads to prevent unwanted seedlings.

OPPOSITE: The unfolding flowerheads of the giant hogweed seem to make a bid for freedom from the papery protective shell that surrounds them.

Hippeastrum (Amaryllidaceae)

amaryllis

Hippeastrums have wonderful flowers. The soft velvety petals of each bloom unfold and combine to form huge sumptuous trumpets in a fanfare of colours. A glorious cluster of blooms is produced on each sturdy stem. They make excellent winter house plants, flowering in the darkest months, with blooms that last for ages.

For maximum impact plant several bulbs of the same colour in a large shallow container. They look spectacular sitting on the floor or decorating a low table. Hippeastrums can also be bought as cut flowers from the florist.

Although the hippeastrum is known universally as the amaryllis, this leads to confusion.

There is a different genus of the same name and, although the flowers look   similar, true amaryllis are half-hardy garden plants from South Africa. The name amaryllis comes from the Ancient Greek for a country girl.

Native to South and Central America, the genus *Hippeastrum* has about 80 species. It was discovered in the Andes in the mid-eighteenth century and in its original wild form it is striped. As with many bulbs, the Dutch have been instrumental in developing the outstanding modern varieties. Favourites of mine include the stunning winter-flowering 'Apple Blossom', which bears white flowers with petals that are blushed with pink; the whitest of white

'Christmas Gift', aptly named because it is a popular present at Christmas and 'Liberty' for its glorious large velvety red flowers. There are other wonderful varieties that offer soft pinks and the original red and white stripes.

With a little care you can keep the bulbs going for years. Cut off the flower stalk when the blooms have faded but carry on watering the plant until autumn. Then move pots to a cool windowsill for a couple of months. To start them into flower again, cut off any remaining foliage and stand them next to a radiator. A cold spell followed by heat makes all the difference, by stimulating bud formation.

Hippeastrums are enormously popular in Greece. Empty feta-cheese containers are whitewashed and filled with these beautiful giants to decorate windowledges and courtyards. There is an intense rivalry as neighbours vie with each other to produce the most spectacular display. I once made the mistake of admiring my next-door neighbour's plants, a whole row of them shining red in the sun. Then I saw her cutting them, I thought for the church. But, alas no, with true Cretan generosity she had cut them for me. I learnt very quickly to be careful about voicing admiration after this, but their rich red-velvet trumpets were the most glorious and humbling bunch of flowers I have ever received.

SOIL CONDITIONS: Rich soil that drains freely. Indoors they thrive on compost that contains loam.
SITUATE: In full sunshine or partial shade.
PROPAGATION: Sow ripe seed.
RESILIENCE: They are not hardy and do not tolerate frost.
CARE: They don't like being disturbed, so only re-pot about every four years or so, in autumn. Watch out for fungus and bulb fly.

LEFT: The pale papery petals of *Hippeastrum* 'Christmas Gift' have a serene presence.
RIGHT: *H.* 'Red Lion', on the other hand, has huge velvety-red trumpets that simply demand attention.

ABOVE: The drooping waxy flowers of the familiar bluebell have a beauty all too often overlooked in comparison with more showy or exotic plants.

Hyacinthoides non-scripta (Hyacinthaceae)

bluebell

The native British bluebell that grows in abundance in woods and coppices is perhaps our best-loved wildflower. Who hasn't stopped and gazed in awe at great drifts of blue, chanced upon while walking in the country, or craned their neck from cars and trains to catch a glimpse? As a child I was told not to pull them up but to pick them carefully, for if ill-treated they would never flower again; I now know it is damage to the foliage (rather than the flowers) that causes their demise.

The bluebell was given the scientific name *Hyacinthoides non-scripta* because, unlike the true hyacinth, its petals do not bear the inscription AI-AI, the Greek of cry of woe (see Hyacinth opposite for a full explanation). Their former name, *Endymion non-scriptus*, recalled the shepherd Endymion, beloved of the Greek moon goddess. She made him fall asleep for ever so that she could caress his body every night. The awesome Unicorn Tapestries, which date back to the early sixteenth century and are now kept in the Cloisters in New York (a branch of the Metropolitan Museum of Art), depict the bluebell alongside periwinkles, lords and ladies and sweet violets, all surrounding the unicorn. In folklore these plants were linked to sexual desire and have come to symbolise fertility.

Bluebells have had many literary plaudits through the centuries. Homer described a drift of bluebells as a 'wine dark sea'. In the thirteenth century the Dominican Friar Daniel wrote that 'many call it daffodil of the wood, for it groweth like daffodil, save he beareth flowers blue-purple.'

Shakespeare wrote of bluebells in his play *Cymbeline*, while Keats and Tennyson lauded them; but my favourite tribute is by the poet Gerard Manley Hopkins in 'The May Magnificat': 'And azuring-over greybell makes, wood banks and brakes wash wet like lakes'.

Bluebells have had other applications, too. The roots were used to make glue in the Middle Ages. They also yielded starch for laundering, similarly to lords and ladies (*Arum maculatum*, see page 24).

Bluebells can be planted under trees and are easily naturalised in wild gardens. I have even seen a painstakingly planted bluebell wood in an Australian private garden, its owner having been inspired by Britain's blue, carpeted woodland.

If you are planning to plant a bluebell wood, make sure of your source of bulbs. The Wildlife and Countryside Act of 1981 made it an offence to dig up bluebells – and any wild plants – without the landowners' express permission. But there are still unscrupulous vandals around who have been known to dig up a complete bluebell wood overnight to sell on to the gardening trade. Buying from a reputable nursery goes some way to helping make sure our heritage is preserved for future generations.

FLOWERING SEASON: Spring.
SOIL CONDITIONS: Soil that does not dry out totally.
SITUATE: In light shade.
PROPAGATION: Divide clumps of bulbs at the end of summer. Seed can be sown in autumn.
RESILIENCE: Hardy.
CARE: Fairly undemanding; can even become invasive.

Hyacinthus (Hyacinthaceae)

hyacinth

The deeply scented hyacinth with its exquisite column of waxen flowers is a sensational plant. It fully deserves its place in history.

In Greek mythology Hyacinthus was a handsome youth much admired by Zephyrus, god of the winds. But Hyacinthus preferred Apollo, so, while they were playing quoits together, Zephyrus deflected one so that it struck Hyacinthus's head and killed him. Apollo, grief-stricken, caused the beautiful hyacinth to grow from the spilt blood. Today each petal still bears the inscription AI-AI, the Ancient Greek cry of woe. Referring to the legend, the great English poet John Milton wrote in *Lycidas*: 'like to that sanguine inscribed with woe'.

Hyacinths grow wild throughout the southeast Mediterranean, in their original colours of violet, blue and white. They were cultivated in Constantinople in the sixteenth century, before arriving in Europe in the second half of the century. John Gerard grew blue-purple and white single hyacinth varieties, but doubles in white, blue and pink were grown elsewhere in Europe.

Eventually the hyacinth joined the ranks of the eight florists' flowers: namely anemones, auriculas, carnations and pinks, primroses, polyanthus, ranunculas and tulips. By the nineteenth century hyacinths had become as collectable as the tulip, resulting in a competitive frenzy in which a single coveted bulb could command the immense price of £100.

For gardeners today, *Hyacinthus amethystinus* (reclassified as *Brimeura amethystina*) from the Spanish Pyrenees, is a good variety to introduce in a wild garden – the white form is particularly beautiful. Resembling the wild bluebell, it has short-stemmed flowers that sit happily under shrubs and grow equally well in woodlands.

H. orientalis, parent of the florists' hyacinth, has an unrivalled perfume. Its star-like bells are delicate pale violet-blue at the base, turning almost white at the spreading lobes. Modern varieties come in shades from white and palest pink to dark purple, through many shades of blue – and even in soft yellows and apricots.

Hyacinths add colour, shape and form to a spring bedding display. Grown indoors they rival any house plant. Why not be bold? Plant lots of bulbs of one colour in huge bowls around the house, and you will be enveloped by their scent. Specially prepared bulbs can be forced to flower in very early spring and, after flowering, can be transplanted to the garden where they will flower in subsequent springs.

Hyacinths will also grow without soil. The Victorians developed hyacinth vases with a wide neck to hold the bulb and a nipped-in waist like an hour-glass to stop it falling into the water below. Children enjoy growing the bulbs in this way, as they can see the emerging roots and slowly unfolding flowers.

FLOWERING SEASON: Spring.
SOIL CONDITIONS: Rich free-draining soil. Use bulb compost indoors.
SITUATE: In a sunny spot.
PROPAGATION: Best left to the experts.
RESILIENCE: Hardy.
CARE: Prone to moulds, rots and insect infestation.

RIGHT: A white form of *Hyacinthus orientalis* is a familiar, yet still impressive, sight in florists' shops.

Hymenocallis (Amaryllidaceae)

spider lily

Lit from behind, the almost translucent white flowers of the hymenocallis are so delicate they seem to be made of paper and, from their form, it is easy to see why the plant is also named the spider lily. The centre of the flower is a cup as fine as a membrane, hence the botanical name *Hymenocallis*, from the Greek *hymen*, meaning fine skin.

There are about 40 species of these bulbous perennials, found in meadows and rocky terrain from the southern parts of the United States to Peru. The flowers are not only extraordinarily beautiful, but also highly perfumed. They do not like frost, although they can be grown with success at the foot of a sheltered wall. Left to their own devices, they bear flowers in profusion and last many years. *Hymenocallis narcissiflora* is the most robust; in summer it bears umbels of up to five headily scented white flowers. Its native habitat is the Andes in Peru and it is the species to try in mild spots in Britain.

The bulbs can be grown in containers and kept indoors for striking house plants. Perhaps it is worth trying *H. caribaea*, for it is a beauty, with evergreen glossy strap-shaped leaves, surmounted by stems of up to ten scented white flowers that bloom from summer to autumn.

I have adored these delicate flowers for years in bouquets from the florist, but I intend to grow some in pots in the house. Then I shall dot them around the garden after the last frosts of spring.

FLOWERING SEASON: Different varieties flower all year round.
SOIL CONDITIONS: Fairly rich free-draining soil. In containers use a compost with a high loam content.
SITUATE: In a protected site either in full sunshine or with some shade.
PROPAGATION: In autumn plant the bulbs with the tops showing.
RESILIENCE: They are susceptible to frost.
CARE: Keep moist. They don't seem to have enemies.

OPPOSITE: *Hymenocallis x festalis* bears extraordinary spidery pure-white flowers that are breathtaking in their beauty.

Iris (Iridaceae)

iris

For me, the most evocative tribute to the iris is from Byron's *Childe Harold's Pilgrimage*: 'From clouds, but of all colours seems to be melted to one vast Iris in the west, where the day joins the past eternity'.

The iris has been revered since ancient times. The Greek goddess Iris used a rainbow as her pathway when she visited earth and the plants that bear her name sprang up wherever she trod. The flowers were depicted in the Minoan Temple at Knossos in Crete, that dates back 2,000 years BC.

The yellow flag *Iris pseudacorus*, which grows wild throughout Europe and the Mediterranean, is almost certainly the biblical lily of the field, since true lilies were not indigenous to the Holy Land. This lily/iris confusion continued until the Middle Ages. In twelfth-century Arabian literature the iris was described as the 'violet lily' in a treatise on its cultivation. A little later it was referred to as 'Irissia – the violet lily' in a work on its medicinal properties.

A strong heraldic symbol, the iris has led kings into battle on more than one occasion. Legend has it that a profusion of yellow flags showed King Clovis I a safe crossing over the River Lys during his battle with the Goths in the sixth century – their presence indicated the water was shallow. He took the yellow flag as his emblem and coined the name fleur-de-lys. King Louis III of France used it as his personal blazon during the Crusades, and when Edward III of England laid claim to the French throne in 1339 it was depicted on his coat of arms with the three Plantagenet lions.

Its name of fleur-de-lys recurs throughout history. In his *New herbal* of 1551 William Turner, an English physician and naturalist, referred to it as 'Flour delice' or 'Fleur deluce', and the herbalist John Parkinson described it in his *Paradisus terrestris* of 1629 as the yellow variable 'Flower de Luce'. History seems to concur that the yellow flag is indeed the fleur-de-lys of France, rather than the lily.

Irises are extraordinarily diverse. The genus includes more than 300 species, from large bearded irises to miniature rockery flowers.

Iris Fiorentina is one of the most ancient plants still in cultivation: the temple of Thutmosis III at Karnak in Egypt is decorated with images of the flower. John Gerard, the sixteenth-century herbalist, stated that from its root 'sweet waters, sweet powders, and suchlike are made'. This ancient practice continues in northern Italy, where iris rhizomes – orris root – are harvested in late summer. They are dried in the sun, often suspended from a line like laundry, then stored for at least two years, when they develop their characteristic violet odour.

Today orris root is chiefly valued for its perfume. In early times it was used to cure a wide range of ailments including scrofula, bronchitis and diarrhoea. A piece of root was often given as a teething ring to babies, while in powder form it was used in snuff and as an inhalant. Its attributes are seemingly endless: orris has also been used for scenting linen and wigs and even to make toothpaste.

The many medicinal properties of the iris caused it to be grown as a curative, but although depicted in art and design, it only began to be planted for its beauty in the early sixteenth century. Since then the iris in all its forms has spread all over the world, its cultivation endlessly evolving.

The history of the bearded iris begins some 350 ago but it was not classified botanically until the early nineteenth century. It is hard to believe that the myriad colours now seen are the result of crossing the powder-blue *I. pallida* and pale yellow *I. variegata*, but dedicated breeders continue to produce all gradations of the spectrum. They hybridise quite freely, which has resulted in an enormous range of varieties. The Americans lead the field in the development of new specimens.

Bearded irises get their name from the hair-like 'beards' on their outer petals. They can be

they make excellent cutting flowers. Many come from China, Korea and Tibet. The stinking iris, *I. foetidissima*, of Europe is also included in this group. It has glossy dark green evergreen foliage with purple flowers, plus the added bonus of bright orange-red seeds, which are revealed in the autumn.

Crested irises hail from North America, Japan and China. They sport a cock's-comb-like crest in the centre of their outer petals that vaguely resembles a beard from a distance.

Bulbous irises came from Persia and are difficult to grow. The Persian iris, *I. persica*, the most fragrant, is also the most tractable. A sheltered spot and a long hot summer is essential. Miniature *I. reticulata* varieties grow from bulbs, too. They are nearly all hardy and make an enchanting addition to rock gardens or as a foreground planting in a border. Forced in pots as a house plant they emit a sweet perfume, and they can be planted out in the garden once they have flowered.

Perhaps the best way to grow and appreciate irises is to provide them with a border of their own. An iris walk is a vision of extraordinary beauty. The choice of varieties is enormous, and to stroll among their wonderful velvety blooms at dawn or dusk, enveloped in their heady scent, is sublime.

sub-divided into dwarf, intermediate and tall forms. The dwarf bearded irises are hardy and bloom in spring. *I. pumila*, an inhabitant of the mountains of south-east Europe, is the first to flower, in shades of yellow and purple, and is an ideal candidate for lighting up a rock garden in mid-spring.

Intermediate bearded irises can be divided further into short and tall forms. Curiously, the timing of their flowers depends on height. Short bearded irises flower earlier than taller ones. The shorter intermediate *I. germanica* is the most common, but there are literally thousands of named varieties of tall bearded irises to choose from. They flower from late spring to mid-summer and, being fully hardy, the knife-like foliage adds height to any planting before and after flowering. They adore the sun, although they were planted in partial shade by the painter Claude Monet in his garden at Giverny in France, because this enhanced the intensity of their colours.

Beardless irises form a large group, all bearing narrow durable and often evergreen foliage, and

FLOWERING SEASON: From the onset of spring to the height of summer.
SOIL CONDITIONS: Fairly rich soil that drains freely, except for water-loving species.
SITUATE: In full sunshine or partial shade.
PROPAGATION: Sow seed of species in pots under glass in both spring and autumn, but it may take years to flower. After flowering, clumps and rhizomes can be divided and replanted.
RESILIENCE: Hardy, but some species are affected by frost.
CARE: Water newly planted irises to help establish a root system. Plant rhizomes on the soil's surface so that they can be baked by the sun in summer. Watch out for snails and slugs.

ABOVE LEFT: *Iris tectorum*, commonly known as the roof iris.
OPPOSITE: *I.* 'Butterscotch', an intermediate bearded iris.

Kniphofia (Asphodelaceae)

red hot poker

The great towers of red kniphofia seem to blaze with heat as they stand triumphant in a border. Kniphofia is named after Johann Hieronymous Kniphof, a professor of medicine at Erfurt in Germany who produced a folio of plant illustrations in 1747. The common names of red hot poker or torch lily are self-explanatory.

Kniphofia is a native of Africa, from the tropics to the south. There are about 70 species; in their natural environment they grow in mountainous regions, particularly alongside streams. The first species to be introduced to Europe was *Kniphofia uvaria in 1707*, but it was the arrival of *K. leichtinii* from Abyssinia in 1880 that resulted in an explosion in popularity. Many hybrids appeared; indeed, they were such treasured members of Victorian gardens that by 1900, there were more than 60.

Most of these have since disappeared. The style police soon banished them to the compost heap, their colours being deemed too strident for fashionable plantings. Today, as 'hot' gardens gain in favour, these noble flowers can shine forth once more. How lucky we are that they have survived. Wherever individualists have refused to be swayed by gardening crazes, old varieties live quietly on. Some of the most inspiring gardens have been planted with love, sensitivity and panache, and little attention to passing fads.

Not all red hot pokers come in bold strident colours. They range from white, verging on soft, green lemons, through the hot part of the spectrum to red. Bees adore them, so it is a good idea to incorporate them in a bee-garden. These tall structural plants are glorious in a summer border or, container grown, they can be moved around smaller gardens at will, filling gaps or adding a splash of colour in dark corners.

I intend to plant *K. northiae*, which bears pale yellow flowers that open from red buds, as a quiet tribute to Marianne North who died in 1890 and whose name they bear. This intrepid traveller and prolific producer of rather odd botanical paintings, which can be seen in her eponymous gallery at Kew Gardens in London, must have been an extraordinary person, and this will be my way of remembering her.

FLOWERING SEASON: From the onset of summer to its very end.
SOIL CONDITIONS: Deep rich freely draining soil with a sand and humus content.
SITUATE: In sunshine with some shade.
PROPAGATION: If grown from seed in pots, sow under glass in spring. Divide large clumps at the beginning of summer.
RESILIENCE: Hardy, but can be frost-prone.
CARE: Protect very young plants with a mulch. Thrips like them.

OPPOSITE: The sculptural shapes of kniphofia are enjoying a revival in popularity today.

In 1817, the poet Keats wrote in his poem 'I stood tip-toe upon a little hill':

'Here are sweet peas, on tip-toe for a flight;
With wings of gentle flush o'er delicate white.'

What could be a better description of these delicate sweetly perfumed flowers? The sweet pea we all know arrived in England in 1699, when some seeds were sent to Dr Robert Uvedale. He was headmaster of Enfield Grammar School in Middlesex, and an eminent botanist. He had one of the first hot-houses in the land, where he nurtured rare exotics. The seeds were sent by Father Franciscus Cupani, a Sicilian monk who had discovered the plant on the island two years earlier. These small plants with maroon and purple blooms proved very popular, and were painted by Redouté, the renowned botanical illustrator of the early nineteenth century.

By the end of the century there were still only six varieties available, the most notable being the 'Painted Lady', which had bicoloured pink and white flowers.

Then Henry Eckford, a plant breeder who had already increased the varieties of dahlias and pansies on sale, discovered that sweet peas are self-pollinating. By cross-pollinating the flowers by hand he raised half of the 264 varieties exhibited at Crystal Palace in 1900. A particular variety he had developed – named 'Lady Nina Balfour', a highly scented soft grey lavender – received all the accolades.

He raised a pale pink variety that he named 'Prima Donna', and sent some seed to a fellow

Lathyrus odoratus (Leguminosae)

sweet pea

gardener, Silas Cole, who tended Countess Spencer's fine gardens at Althorp Park in Northamptonshire. From that batch grew a rogue plant with large frilled petals. Silas Cole named it 'Countess Spencer', and to this day all waved varieties are referred to as Spencers.

Almost simultaneously a grocer, one W. J. Unwin in Cambridge, noticed a frilled sweet pea in his garden. He named this after his daughter Gladys, left the grocery trade, and had great success growing sweet peas for the cut-flower market before setting up a seed-merchant business that is still flourishing today.

Sweet peas have been grown in cottage gardens ever since. The traditional way of planting them was in the kitchen garden, using the wires of wall-grown espaliered fruit trees for them to scramble up, where they adore baking in hot sun. This method takes a lot of beating, but we don't all have a walled garden. They look wonderful clambering over a fence of twiggy sticks or wattle, creating a gently coloured wall to give a garden some structure. They grow up tripods with style and can enhance a vegetable garden.

Allotment holders grow them up wires and bamboo canes, to cut for the home. The more they are picked, the more flowers they produce, only stopping if seedpods are allowed to set.

Enthusiasts who grow Spencer sweet peas as exhibition flowers train them up a cane, pinching out side shoots and tendrils, to endow the plants with strength to produce straight long-stemmed blooms. The old-fashioned varieties, those that most closely resemble the original wild Sicilian sweet pea, don't respond so well to this rigorous treatment and are best grown in tumbling masses.

There are the most exquisite colours to choose from: you can be tasteful and grow a mass of one colour, or flamboyant with a mix of all shades. They are marvellous garden flowers, long-lasting, prolific, and providing ever more bunches of flowers for the home, with enough over to give to visitors. There is nothing more delightful than visiting industrious friends and leaving with a bunch of freshly picked flowers. They are so much more welcome than a bouquet from the florist – however luxurious – for these have been tended and cherished by people you know.

FLOWERING SEASON: From the onset of summer to the end of autumn.
SOIL CONDITIONS: Rich soil that drains freely, preferably with added humus.
SITUATE: In sunshine.
PROPAGATION: In spring sow seed in pots under glass. Seed can be sown in the required spot in the garden in autumn.
RESILIENCE: Mostly hardy but tender growth can be cut down by late frosts.
CARE: Provide support and pick freely for a continuous display. Aphids and pollen beetles can be a nuisance.

BELOW: A charming tangle of pastel-coloured everlasting pea (*Lathyrus latifolius*).
OPPOSITE: *L. odoratus* 'Wiltshire Ripple' has the bold colouring and straight stems of a modern variety.

ABOVE: Lavender fields flourish on the island of Jersey.
OPPOSITE: The flowerheads of *Lavandula angustifolia* 'Twickel Purple'.

Lavandula (Labiatae)

lavender

Lavender deserves a place in nearly every garden, for its gentle blues permeate a border like a mist, and envelop it in the most soothing of perfumes. A few heads pulled in passing can be crushed and enjoyed in the still of the evening, when the garden becomes a place of rest and not a taskmaster.

Lavender is named from *lavare*, the Latin verb to wash. A native plant of southern Europe and the Mediterranean, it has been known for centuries. The Romans used it for its perfume and in baths, and almost certainly took it with them on their travels. It is first recorded in England in medieval times, although it is thought to have arrived with the Romans. In Elizabethan times, when not much bathing occurred, a laundress was known as a 'lavandre' and lavender was used to perfume both clothes and bed linen.

Lavender was greatly used as a strewing herb in the malodorous past, and large dishes containing the dried flowers were placed at the hearth, handfuls being thrown on the embers to perfume the room. The powerful aroma of lavender is said to discourage mice and vermin, and bunches placed in rooms deter flies and mosquitoes. John Gerard, the sixteenth-century herbalist, remarked that powdered lavender, mixed with cinnamon, nutmeg and cloves, helped 'the panting and passion of the heart, prevaileth against giddiness, turning or swimming of, the brain'. It was also used as a diuretic, calmer of colic and vermifuge.

Today a few drops of lavender oil can be used to make a healing mouthwash if added to a glass of water, to soothe aches and pains when massaged into joints, and to calm the nerves like a gentle sedative. A few drops of oil on a pillow is not only heavenly to smell, it also helps to induce sleep.

Another use of this invaluable aromatic is in perfume and soap. The purple lavender fields of Provence are the most glorious sight, and the air is heavy with scent at harvest time. Essence of lavender is costly, but just a few drops go a long way. It is an important ingredient of pot-pourri, while sewn in muslin bags it perfumes lingerie and linen, and is a deterrent to moths. As a reluctant child seamstress, I dutifully made lavender bags for aged aunts, to be given as Christmas presents. Placed in an airing cupboard among the linen, they gently perfume the whole space.

Easy to cultivate, lavender is wonderful in the garden and the small varieties are invaluable in establishing fast-growing parterres and knot gardens. Great blocks enclosed by low wattle fences are spectacular: the recreated medieval garden at the Prieuré d'Orsan in the Berry region of France is a fine example. Lavender is also a perfect foil for roses. At its zenith, lavender hums with bees and is aquiver with butterflies.

I have grown great pots full in my courtyard, the silver foliage remaining winter long, tolerant of neglect. Kept in pots on a window ledge, it forms a gentle screen, suffusing the room with its fragrance.

Lavandula stoechas, known in the sixteenth century as stickadore, grows in great drifts in the Atlas Mountains in Morocco, its soft deep purple dappling the mountainsides. A handsome plant, with large coloured tufted bracts on each flowered head, it is not fully hardy in northern Europe but can be grown with success in a sheltered position or in a pot that can be shifted into a cool greenhouse for the winter. Broad-leaved *L. lanata*, introduced from Spain in Regency times, lives contentedly sheltering against walls, and has flowers of a rich purple.

Perfumed gardens are an antidote to the flurry of modern life. Sitting in quiet contemplation at the end of the day, amid an oasis of lavender-scented tranquillity, is succour to both mind and spirit.

FLOWERING SEASON: From summer through until the autumn.
SOIL CONDITIONS: Rich to fairly rich soil that drains freely.
SITUATE: In sunshine.
PROPAGATION: Sow in pots under glass in spring. Cuttings can be taken in summer.
RESILIENCE: Hardy to half-hardy.
CARE: If drying the flowers, harvest while still in bud for more scent. Can be susceptible to botrytis.

Lilium (Liliaceae)

lily

The deeply scented lily is in a class of its own. Its seductive trumpets emit an entrancing perfume that can fill a room – or a garden. And it is rivalled only by the rose in antiquity. Symbolising grace and purity, its image has been used since the beginning of recorded history by artists, poets and authors.

The purest of the species is undoubtedly *Lilium candidum*, the Madonna lily, with its gentle perfume. The Minoan civilisation in Crete used it as a motif more than any other flower. It was sacred to Britomartis, the mother goddess. Passed down to Hera, the later Greek goddess of marriage and childbirth, it was then adopted by the Romans, who dedicated it to Juno, from whose milk the flowers are said to spring. Both the Greeks and the Romans used lilies in marriage crowns, a tradition still observed today in bridal bouquets.

The Moors, admiring of the lily's symmetry, planted it wherever they went, and with the arrival of Christianity it became synonymous with the Virgin Mary. It is believed to have finally reached Britain via the Romans.

Its medicinal uses seem few, though the Ancient Greeks pounded the bulbs to a paste to be used as a balm for skin diseases, and mixed with honey it became a wrinkle-reducing face-pack. In medieval rural England the petals were used to heal cuts, either as a decoction or applied as a poultice.

The Madonna lily was almost the lone lily species until the late sixteenth century, when new ones arrived from Europe, Turkey and America. But the real explosion happened with

LEFT AND ABOVE: *Lilium candidum* (left) has pink-flushed petals that are restful to contemplate, while red lilies (above) make a bold statement in a border.

the influx of lilies from the Far East in the nineteenth century. The tiger lily (*L. tigrinium*, now referred to as *L. lancifolium*), from Canton in 1804 and *L. speciosum* from Japan in 1832 were notable examples. *L. martagon*, the purple Turk's cap lily, was popular in the sixteenth century, while *L. chalcedonicum*, the scarlet Turk's cap lily from Greece and Turkey, shot to fame in the seventeenth century, (though it was definitely grown earlier by John Gerard, who knew it as 'the red lily of Constantinople').

FLOWERING SEASON: From the onset of summer until its close.

SOIL CONDITIONS: Soil that drains freely, preferably with added leafmould, but they are tolerant.

SITUATE: In sunshine and dappled shade. Underplant to keep sunshine from their base.

PROPAGATION: Seed from species should be sown in pots when ripe, under glass. Plant bulbs in the garden in autumn at a depth of about twice their height as a general rule. Stem-rooting lilies need planting deeper.

RESILIENCE: Hardy but with some varieties prone to frost.

CARE: Tall varieties may need support. Slugs and snails love them, as does the lily beetle.

The lily continued to be a familiar garden plant but was not grown with such fervour as some fashionable flowers. However, the introduction of *L. auratum* from Japan, shown with great success at the Royal Horticultural Show of 1862, rekindled interest – as well it might, with its stunning gold and white flowers up to 25cm (10in) across, carried ten to a stem.

Given the right conditions, lilies thrive throughout the temperate regions of the northern hemisphere. Virtually every self-respecting cottage garden boasts a display, although these are generally the easily grown and tolerant *L. regale* from Tibet, introduced in 1904. They like to be left in peace and will then obligingly bloom for years. Lilies enjoy the company of other plants because they like their roots to be shaded. The tall stems have impressive stature and form, and since different species and varieties bloom for most of the summer, you can keep a succession of flowers coming.

In medieval times, in the paradise gardens arranged for contemplation and meditation, *L. candidum* held pride of place. These gardens, with their turf seats, pergolas and walkways, can be easily reconstructed today, either as a 'room' within a large garden, or as a whole in a small space. To sit on a turf seat in an arbour in the cool of a summer evening surrounded by lilies is reward enough for the labour involved.

The wonderful garden at Bois de Moutier in Varengeville, Normandy, which was designed by Gertrude Jekyll, has an inspired planting of *L. candidum* mixed with bronze fennel, a joyous combination. With their height and grace, lilies complement any border. They also grow happily in pots and make glorious house plants for the garden-deprived city dweller, filling the room with their heady fragrance.

OPPOSITE: *Lilium longiflorum* supplies ideal cut flowers, although you should avoid brushing past them as the pollen stains clothes.

Meconopsis (Papavaeraceae)

Himalayan poppy

BELOW: *Meconopsis betonicifolia* has petals of royal-blue crêpe.
RIGHT: *M. napaulensis* flourishes in cool moist gardens.

The pellucid blue of the Himalayan poppy has enchanted gardeners ever since its discovery. Like a leading soprano, it delicately highlights wherever it is planted and its clarity of colour is perfect. Its name comes from the Greek *mekon* (poppy) and *opsis* (like). The species *Meconopsis grandis* was discovered in Sikkim in north-east India, close to the Tibetan border, in the late nineteenth century. For some time this was thought to be the only site where the plants grew, but it was later discovered in Tibet and Nepal, although in slightly different form. The plant can be tall, and with its large saucer-shaped blooms of the most electrifying blue, it is stunning. There is a form from Bhutan that is even taller and bears several large blooms.

One variety discovered in 1933 became known during the 1940s as 'Betty Sheriff's Dream Poppy'. When accompanying her husband, the renowned plant hunter George Sheriff, on a Himalayan expedition, Mrs Betty Sheriff stayed behind alone while he travelled elsewhere. In a dream she had while he was away he told her where to look for a new poppy. The next morning, by following these directions, she found the poppy. Writing to her husband to find out if telepathy had been involved, she received the reply that he had been thinking neither of her nor the poppy.

To a layman like me, the most easily spotted

difference between meconopsis and other poppies – apart from their colour – is that the seedhead is a long thin ovoid, without the disc-like top that characterises the seedhead of other members of the poppy family.

Meconopsis are distributed over a vast area of the Himalayas, experiencing great climatic changes. We owe a huge vote of thanks to the dedicated plant-hunting expeditions of mountaineers, botanists and enthusiastic amateurs who brought new forms to the West that still grow in our gardens.

Meconopsis can be grown most successfully in areas that match their natural habitat – Scotland is ideal, for example. What they need is cool moisture and Scotland's annual rainfall is just about adequate. But with care they can be grown elsewhere. The collection at The Savill Garden in Windsor Great Park near London proves this with some style.

They are easily hybridised, achieving many different colours, but the results are often sterile. For me, blue reigns supreme. No one can be unmoved by the rich hues of the perennial *M. grandis*. Blue flowers are always magical, beloved of both plantsmen and gardeners. It is certainly a challenge, but a great drift of azure in dappled shade is hard to beat. Rock-garden enthusiasts can try the small alpine species.

By selecting species carefully the normal flowering season, from the beginning of spring through to summer, can be stretched until summer's end. Meconopsis may be difficult and quixotic, but with care and attention they can be a glorious reward for the effort expended.

FLOWERING SEASON: From the end of spring throughout the summer.
SOIL CONDITIONS: Rich soil that drains freely, preferably with added humus.
SITUATE: Dappled shade.
PROPAGATION: When ripe, seeds should be sown in pots under glass. Large clumps can be divided when they have finished flowering.
RESILIENCE: They are hardy.
CARE: Young growth should be protected from the cold, and given water and a mulch during a hot summer. Beware slugs.

Molucella (Labiateae)

bells of Ireland

The soft green, almost translucent 'bells' of this plant endow it with great charm. What at first appear to be flowers are, in fact, papery-green calyxes, which protect the small white flowers within. The main species, *Molucella laevis*, is one of a small group of annual and briefly surviving perennial plants numbering only four species in total. Its habitat is poor ground from the north-west of India to the Mediterranean. The plants used to be common in the gardens of the nineteenth century but are rarely grown today, though I detect something of a revival in their popularity.

They look splendid as additions to a herbaceous border. Green can be a useful ingredient in a planting scheme, creating a pause and resting place for the eye. Bells of Ireland do not grow to great heights, so are fine for the mid-point in a bed, which is often difficult to fill. An annual border is enhanced by their inclusion, and any flower that can be cut then kept for a long time indoors has to be worth while. These qualities ensure the cut stems are usually on sale in high-street florists – and the fresh flowers are easily dried for winter arrangements.

FLOWERING SEASON: Summer flowering, but they last well into autumn.
SOIL CONDITIONS: Fairly rich soil that drains freely.
SITUATE: In an open sunny spot.
PROPAGATION: Sow in the garden at the end of spring.
RESILIENCE: They are not completely hardy.
CARE: Self-sufficient.

OPPOSITE: The green cup-shaped calyxes of *Molucella laevis* seem to cradle its insignificant white flowers.

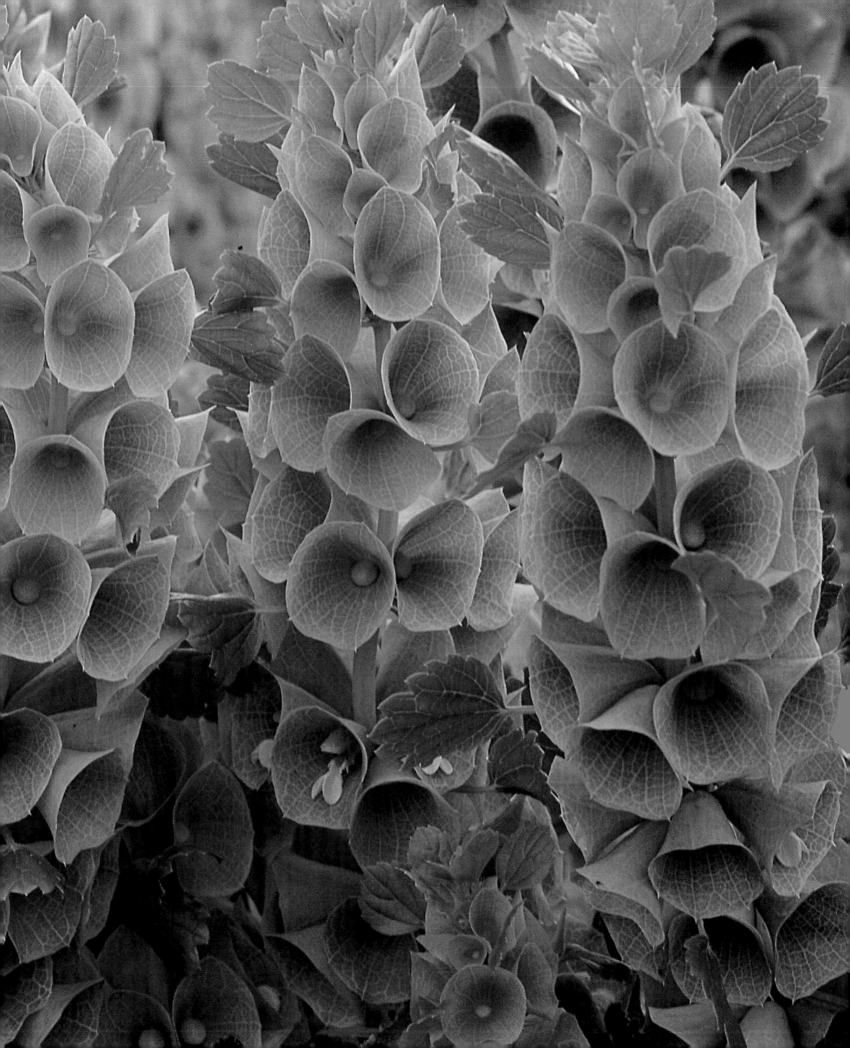

Musa (Musaceae)

banana

A beautiful garden I visited in Key West, Florida, had bananas growing as specimen plants. Towering above terrestrial orchids and dwarfed by immense palms, they were spectacular – both bawdy and beautiful.

As well as looking ornamental, the banana is one of the world's most important food crops. Banana is the native name of the fruit in Guinea in Africa, while *musa* is its Arabic name. The banana thrives throughout the tropics and 40 species are found at the forest's edge in Bangladesh and the north-east of India. They also grow in the north of Australia, Japan and south-eastern Asia. Not only is the banana good to eat, the paddle-like leaves are used to thatch roofs, as a wrapping for food cooked slowly in charcoal pits and, finally, as serving plates.

Bananas were known to Alexander the Great, who saw them growing in India. Soon after the discovery of America the banana was introduced to the New World from the Canary Islands. It was first established as a crop on Hispaniola and was quickly taken up on other islands and eventually the mainland. By the early nineteenth century bananas were being sold in the markets of America.

The most widely grown of the species is *Musa sapientum*, which is eaten fresh, dried, mashed – in fact in almost any guise – for it is a staple for many people. A large stately plant, it grows easily in the right habitat, producing its first fruit within a year; with judicious pruning it goes on to bear fruit almost continuously.

The flower is an extraordinary sight. It is large and produced at the top of the plant. As it is so heavy, it bends downwards, eventually bearing up to 150 fruit, which grow in the hand-like bunches that we all know. A large quantity of fruit can be produced on a small area of land, which makes bananas such a valuable and worthwhile crop. They can be raised in a large hot-house in less suitable climes, but for most of us they are to be eaten only. Some brave gardeners grow them in temperate regions but they have to be swathed in protective fleece to survive the winter.

I was extremely surprised when I walked into my local florist and saw dwarf fruiting flowers for sale. The florist trade never ceases to amaze me: now it's possible to buy exotic plants from all over the world at affordable prices, while our forebears had to risk life and limb to discover these former rarities.

FLOWERING SEASON: Summer flowering.
SOIL CONDITIONS: Outdoors they need rich soil with a high humus content. Indoors use a compost that contains loam.
SITUATE: In full sun.
PROPAGATION: Sow the seed when it is ripe. Large clumps can be divided after four years.
RESILIENCE: They are susceptible to frost.
CARE: Shelter them from the wind. Either bring plants in before the frosts begin, or wrap them and leave in situ in a very sheltered spot.

OPPOSITE: Banana plants make amazing specimens, looking exotic almost to the point of embarrassment.

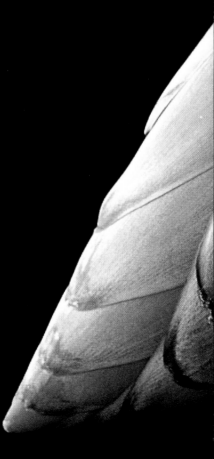

Narcissus (Amaryllidaceae)

pheasant's eye

Perfect in its purity and sweetly perfumed, the narcissus is worthy of its legendary status. The story of Narcissus, whose name has entered our language via narcissism or self-adoration, tells of a handsome young man who fell in love with his reflection in a pool of water. He leaned over, fell into the water and drowned. One ending to the tale has Aphrodite turning him into a flower because of his vanity; another has the nymphs coming to find his body (which had vanished), leaving the beautiful narcissus growing where he had lain. As a result the flower forever dips its head, to see its own reflection. Despite the obvious connection between legend and flower,

the botanical name is thought actually to have come from the Greek *narkau*, to become stiff or numb, for the bulbs are said to be narcotic.

The Ancient Egyptians used Narcissi in funeral wreaths and to decorate tombs, as did the Ancient Greeks. In some countries they are still unwelcome in the house because of these connotations.

The pheasant's eye (*Narcissus poeticus*) has been grown in Britain since the time of the Tudors and has become naturalised in some parts of south-east England. The perfume that these beauties possess is exquisite. When they are grown in pots in the house they fill the room

with their heady scent. They also make wonderful cutting flowers, planted in rows in a corner of the vegetable plot, maybe, so that you don't feel you are stripping the garden of vital blooms when you pick them.

FLOWERING SEASON: Late in spring.
SOIL CONDITIONS: They like moisture when growing.
SITUATE: They can tolerate some shade later in the year when growth has finished.
PROPAGATION: Plant bulbs at a depth of three times their height.
RESILIENCE: Hardy.
CARE: Water in dry weather.

BELOW AND OPPOSITE: The papery blooms of *N. poeticus* look enchanting both in close-up and when naturalised in spring meadows.

Nerine (Amaryllidaceae)

nerine

Great clusters of feathery nerine trumpets lift their heads proudly in autumn, giving a passable impression of spring. The flowers have a delicacy often missing at this time of year when the garden is preparing itself for winter.

The autumn-flowering nerine is named from Nereid, the Greek water-nymph. There are 30 species of this bulbous perennial, found on mountainsides, rocky outcrops and dry areas in their native habitat in southern Africa. Some are fairly robust, and can be grown in areas that do not have too many frosts. Planted at the foot of a sheltering wall, each stem can bear up to 25 flowers each, arranged in a loose sphere. The low curving leaves follow later.

Nerine bowdenii is a fine example and also the hardiest. It bears elegant pink flowers in autumn that are lightly scented. *N. sarniensis* and *N. undulata* can be grown in mild areas. *N. sarniensis*, the Guernsey lily, flowers at the onset of autumn with heads of up to 20 flowers, with petals of orange to the brightest crimson, and elegant long stamens. *N. undulata* has delicately tapering flowers of a soft pink. There are other varieties, from white through to red, with every shade of pink inbetween.

As with many slightly delicate bulbs, nerines come into their own as container plants. They like to be constricted, so life in a pot genuinely suits them. They can sit outside until the first frosts descend and then be brought inside.

Nerines also make long-lasting cut flowers, and add grace to any arrangement; on their own they look simply beautiful.

In my cottage garden in Norfolk I have watched a traditional countryman's choice of flowers emerge throughout the summer. I was delighted to find delicate pink nerines blossoming in a sheltered bed as autumn approached. If they can withstand the rigours of a Norfolk winter, I would imagine they can survive almost anywhere in Britain.

FLOWERING SEASON: Early to late autumn.
SOIL CONDITIONS: Soil that drains freely.
SITUATE: In full sunlight.
PROPAGATION: Sow seeds in pots in a glass coldframe when they are ripe. Plant bulbs in either spring or autumn with their necks exposed, using a compost that contains loam.
RESILIENCE: Some are hardy, some are frost-prone.
CARE: Bulbs like to be crowded. Keep moist when growing, warm and dry while dormant. Outside they should be mulched in cold weather. Watch out for slugs.

BELOW: *Nerine bowdenii* 'Mark Fenwick'.

Nidularium (Bromeliaceae)

bromeliad

The strange quality of the bromeliad, which on first sight appears to be rather hostile with its hard spiny foliage, becomes attractive when it is seen in profusion in its natural habitat. It is an exotic beast, bringing form and colour to desert and dry gardens. Bromeliads are so determined to survive that they are well nigh self-sufficient – a wonderful example of nature's life force.

There are more than 40 species in this varied group, which contains evergreens, as well as terrestrial and epiphytic perennials. In frost-free regions they are ideal for including in a desert garden, but elsewhere raise them in containers of gritty compost and keep them above freezing – move them outdoors to a sunny position only for the summer. Bromeliads also make excellent house plants that can be enjoyed all year.

Linnaeaus named bromeliads after Olaus Bromel, a fellow Swede, in 1753. The most famous member of the family is the pineapple, which was discovered in Guadaloupe by Christopher Columbus. The number of known family members was further increased by the Belgians who collected specimens from Brazil.

A collection of bromeliads was established at Kew Gardens in London in 1785. Although bromeliads were virtually unknown outside continental Europe before 1950, the fledgling Bromeliad Society based in California has spread the word, so that there are now collections of importance in Australia, North America and South Africa. The enthusiasm displayed by the

RIGHT: Bromeliads are almost self-sufficient, using their flowers to trap rainwater.

collectors of these bizarre looking plants is highly infectious.

Last year we made a pilgrimage to see a private collection at Trinity Beach in Queensland, Australia, where an amazing display of these plants can be seen. The garden features many rare plants, but the owner's great love is the bromeliad. He doesn't believe in watering because water is a scarce resource, but the bromeliads thrive on practically no rain at all and his lawns come green immediately after rain. Australia is a constant reminder of nature in the raw, where the doughty inhabitants battle with drought, fire and poisonous creatures, yet continue to create the most wonderful gardens.

SOIL CONDITIONS: Well-drained loam ideally but they will survive in any soil.
SITE: Sunny position sheltered from cold winds.
PROPAGATION: In spring from seeds or cuttings.
RESILIENCE: Hardy if not displaced – they can live for 50 years.
CARE: Protect first shoots from frost, mulch annually in spring and water in dry weather.

RIGHT: Bromeliads are survivors, clinging to the least hospitable site with a fierce determination.

Nigella (Ranunculaceae)

love-in-a-mist

An essential ingredient in a cottage garden, nigella or love-in-a-mist is a feathered enchantress. Its limpid delicate flowers are wreathed in a mist of tendrils of the softest green, creating a gentle haze wherever they are planted. Nigella is named from the latin *niger*, meaning black, which refers to the seeds of *Nigella sativa*, a cottage-garden plant since Elizabethan times. The name love-in-a-mist has a more earthy association, referring to the fine hair-like leaves that surround the flowers. Slightly less euphemistically, the French call them *cheveux de Venus*. Nigella is also known as devil-in-a-bush.

There are 20 species native to poor soil in north Africa, the Mediterranean and Central Asia. *N. sativa* was grown as a crop in Ancient Egypt: the seeds were used for flavouring bread and cakes, and women ate them because they believed they would enhance the size of their breasts. The plant was also known as Roman coriander or black cumin. The finely ground seeds were useful for ridding the hair of lice, while inhaled as a snuff they were said to restore the sense of smell.

In Tudor times nigella seeds were known as giths, and were used as both a delouser and an aromatic. The seeds were placed in fine cotton bags, then warmed and inhaled. The bags were also hung near the fire, suffusing the room with their delicious perfume as they grew warm.

In Italy and France nigella was also known as the nutmeg plant and the seeds were used to flavour cheeses. An aromatic oil was also produced from the seeds, a cheaper version of the costly Indian spikenard, which it resembles.

N. sativa is not widely grown today, having been superseded by *N. damascena*, supposedly hailing from Damascus. In the sixteenth century, John Gerard wrote of them that 'the wild ones do grow of themselves among corn'. *N. damascena* has more of the delightful mist surrounding its delicate blue flower. Another lovely plant is *N. hispanica*, *bearing* flowers of a rich blue with stamens of the deepest red. *N. orientalis* has unusual single yellow flowers.

Whichever species you grow, these charming dainty flowers impart the most beautiful tracery to a flowerbed. They look superb when nestling under pink roses. They are vigorous self-seeding annuals and will thrive on being thinned out, when they become much sturdier. Even the seedheads are extremely decorative, and can be left in the flower border or dried for the house.

These fragile flowers have been with us for centuries, enhancing gardens with their delicate clear colours, and they deserve to remain there.

SOIL CONDITIONS: They are tolerant but prefer soil that drains freely.
SITUATE: In full sunshine.
PROPAGATION: Sow seed in the required place in the garden in both spring and autumn.
RESILIENCE: Hardy.
CARE: Self-sufficient.

BELOW: The feathery tracery of love-in-a-mist makes it a welcome addition to a garden scheme.

Nymphaea (Nymphaeaceae)

water lily

The glorious water lily is distributed widely throughout the world in ponds, lakes and still waters. The genus is named after Nympha, the virgin water-nymph of Ancient Greece and at dawn and dusk the flowers do look like wraiths in the half-light.

Water lilies are of great antiquity. The Ancient Egyptians revered them and depicted them in their art. Water lilies adorned the statue of Osiris and were included in offerings to the dead. Petals were found in the funeral wreath of Rameses II when his tomb was excavated.

The Ancient Greeks believed water lilies were an anti-aphrodisiac. The monks and nuns of the Middle Ages maintained this belief, making pastes of the ground lilies mixed with honey to help preserve their celibacy – though no one is very sure exactly how they were used.

The water lily family consists of 50 species. The common white water lily *Nymphaea alba* is the only one native to the British Isles. The most spectacular species is the enormous *Victoria amazonica*, which allegedly caused the nineteenth-century botanical explorer Aimé Bonpland to fall into the water with surprise on seeing it in its natural habitat.

The plant was first grown in England in 1849, when Joseph Paxton, gardener to the Duke of Devonshire, was responsible for the construction of the tank that contained it. Its vast ribbed leaves gave him the inspiration for his famed designs for Crystal Palace, built for the Great exhibition of 1851.

A flower was presented to Queen Victoria and named *Victoria regina* in her honour. But it was subsequently discovered that Eduard Poeppig, the explorer, had already named the plant *Euryale amazonica* in 1832 after one of the three Gorgons of Greek myth. Even though botanists decided it was not to be a member of the euryale family and could be called *Victoria amazonica* it was still deemed inappropriate to reveal its botanical name to the queen because the Amazon connection was considered to be unseemly. The Latin name was kept secret until her death, and decorum was preserved.

Monsieur Bory Latour-Marliac, known as the Father of the Water Lily, of Temple-sur-Lot in southern France, raised new water lily hybrids starting with *N.* 'Marliacea Rosea' in 1897. These are immortalised in Claude Monet's paintings of the water lilies in his garden at Giverny. We have France to thank for the great choice of the beautiful hardy water lilies that grace our gardens today.

The USA is in the forefront of developing tropical varieties of water lilies, and American breeders carry out their search for perfection with typical enthusiasm. There is a generous choice of water lilies readily available, although it is worth seeking out the specialist for the more obscure varieties.

Few people have vast expanses of still water in their garden, but there are water lilies to suit all circumstances. The hardiest have a vast colour range, from the purest white, soft yellow, pink and apricot through to the deepest red. Some

OPPOSITE: *Nymphaea* 'General Pershing' has narrower petals than many other varieties of water lily.

flowers change colour as they age. These wonderful flowers of flawless purity usually open and close with the sun, their dark green leaves contrasting with the blooms to make them sharp highlights of colour.

The North American *N. tuberosa* opens in the afternoon and some species bloom only at night – but these are mostly frost-tender plants.

Water lilies despise fountains and running water, but can be grown with ease in still water almost anywhere. The Chinese grow them in large pots in their gardens. Small varieties will even survive in a washing-up bowl and *N. capensis zanzibariensis*, with rich blue scented flowers, can be grown indoors. Water in the garden induces a sense of peace and tranquillity, and even the smallest garden can usually encompass a tiny pond somewhere. The combination of glossy green leaves and starry flowers is unsurpassed. For those with no cats or herons, a flicker of fish under the plants brings another dimension altogether, creating a recipe for contemplation, much needed in these hectic times.

FLOWERING SEASON: From the middle of summer to its close.
SOIL CONDITIONS: Under water in firm soil that contains loam. Use a mesh basket to plant them in.
SITUATE: In full sunshine in still water.
PROPAGATION: Seed should be sown when ripe, and some species self-seed. Divide hybrid plants in the autumn.
RESILIENCE: They range from hardy to susceptible to frost.
CARE: Submerge in shallow water at first, gradually increasing the depth as they mature.

OPPOSITE: The creamy symmetrical blooms of *Nymphaea* 'Alba'.

Orchis (Orchidaceae)

orchid

The sensuously exotic orchid has been coveted in all its myriad forms. From the humble terrestrial orchids of the Mediterranean and temperate regions to the sumptuous beauties of the tropical rainforest, man has long been beguiled by their seductive glamour. There is an enormous variety of hybrids and species: some are epiphytic and live on other plants, while deriving their nutrients from rainfall and the air; lithophytic varieties grow on rocks; and the remainder are terrestial or ground-growing.

In the first century AD Dioscorides described wild kunorchis plants as 'dogs testicles' – the word *orchis* meaning testicle in Ancient Greek. These wild orchids were dedicated to satyrs and sileni: part-human, part-animal attendants to the wine god Dionysus, they were lustful creatures who caroused through Arcadia.

The tubers of terrestrial orchids do resemble testicles of unequal sizes. They have one full tuber, a food store for the next year's growth, and a shrivelled one that supplies the current year's nutrients. The women of Thessaly used to steep the tubers in goats' milk: the full tuber was used as an aphrodisiac, the shrivelled one for the very opposite effect. They also believed that if a man ate the larger tuber he would father a boy, and if a woman ate the smaller one she would conceive a girl.

The use of orchid tubers has continued. When steeped in water they produce an easily digestible substance called salep. In winter the cafes of Istanbul still serve it as a hot nourishing drink and street vendors exhort passers-by to stop and buy, with cries of 'salep, salep, salep'. Plundered for their use as love potions, too, terrestrial orchids have seriously declined in the wild. As recently as 1970, more than 2,000kg were exported from Turkey.

The ravishing sirens of the tropical rain-forest have suffered a similar history of plunder. Perhaps the most famous one is the vanilla orchid, the seed-pod of which was used by the Aztecs to flavour their chocolate – a practice viewed with some suspicion at first by Old World explorers. Yet vanilla is now one of the most ubiquitous food flavourings.

Orchids didn't really gain popularity until the mid-eighteenth century, when Linnaeus listed 69 species. By the nineteenth century they were being sought throughout the world. Great tracts of forest were felled and collectors sent hundreds of thousands of plants back to England, many of them perishing on the way – as did some of the collectors.

In their native environment orchids truly are jewels beyond belief. Under the canopy of the rainforest, surrounded by steamy air, they hang from trees, sending their tendril-like roots earthwards but in fact living on air.

There are avid orchid societies all over the world. In Florida, where orchids grow with ease, there is enormous enthusiasm. I visited a private garden on a dock in one of the Florida Keys to see the most amazing collection. Orchids hung from trees, grew on logs, swung from baskets, each one more enchanting than the last. The forms are endless, from tiny delicate blooms in the softest of shades to great lush strident chorus girls of flowers, shouting their frilly beauty from the tree tops. It is very easy to become infatuated and embark on a love affair.

Even those of us in cooler climes without a hot-house can still enjoy orchids at home. They are available as pot plants from most florists, costing little more than the price of a bunch of flowers, yet lasting far longer.

Look out for cymbidium orchids, which are popular as house plants. They have yellowy-green flowers with a splash of red, surrounded by a ruff of green sepals. Plants can send up flower spikes up to 1m (3ft) long with as many as 20 flowers per stem.

Some orchids sold for the home are scented. Dendrobium has yellow sweetly scented flowers that are produced in winter through to spring. Coelogyne flowers at the same time, sending up stems of fragrant white blooms splashed with yellow. Like most rainforest species, all three of these orchids are epiphytic.

Nowadays, with more responsible attitudes towards conservation, orchids can be sourced and bought blamelessly, in the knowledge that they have been grown by specialists, not wrenched from their native habitat.

Orchid
This vast collection of
differing species has
equally differing require-
ments. Terrestrial
orchids can be natu-
ralised in damp mead-
ows, and enjoy the
shade, but can also be
grown in a greenhouse.
Epiphytic orchids can be
grown on trees and
pieces of bark. They
need humidity and
warmth. Lithophytic
varieties are happy in a
rock garden in the right
climate. In Europe most
orchids, except the
tough native varieties,
need to be grown in a
hot-house. Gardeners in
tropical climates can
grow them with ease, of
course.

Tree orchid
These can be grown on
bark or in special
compost. They need
feeding and moisture.
Grow them out of direct
sunlight and spray with
a fine mist of water
every day.

RIGHT AND OVERLEAF:
The delicacy of some of
the terrestrial varieties
of orchid (right) is far
removed from the exotic
extravagance of tropical
varieties (overleaf).

Paeonia (Paeoniaceae)

peony

The great exuberant cups of the peony not only please the eye, but perfume the air. They are resplendent in a garden; their shaggy heads radiate colour, so that although they have but a brief flowering season, they are well worth planting. The peony is one of the few perennials still grown that was recorded by the Ancients. Its name is derived from that of Paeon, physician to the gods in Greek mythology, who was the first to use the plant for its medicinal properties – he used it to heal the gods Hades and Ares after a battle. Although the species of peony have evolved since then, there are still essentially just two distinct sorts – the tree peony and the herbaceous peony. Both have their origins in the East, though certain species of herbaceous peony are also endemic in Europe. Species such as *Paeonia mascula* and *P. officinalis,* which now grow all over Europe, East Asia and western North America, were revered on the island of Crete and can be traced back as far as the Minoan civilisation.

In medieval times *P. mascula*, together with *P. officinalis*, was treasured by royalty and the Church, and deemed an essential plant in both physick and paradise gardens. It was tended by monks all over Europe for its medicinal qualities: its dried roots were said to cure epilepsy, convulsions and even lunacy. Like the mandrake the peony was thought to be imbued with fearsome magical powers. Knowledge of flowers and plants was still at this time largely based on the works of Theophrastus and Pliny, and they both recommended that it should be gathered only at night, as picking it in the daytime was dangerous (it was believed it could cause madness). This superstition may have arisen from the fact that the seeds of some species are phosphorescent and shine eerily in the dark.

The peony's reputation as a curative survived into the nineteenth century, when the roots were still being worn by children to prevent epilepsy, and compound peony water was taken for nervous disorders. The English also appreciated peonies for their taste, using them to flavour roast pork. In folklore, however, peonies were seen as harbingers of doom. An odd number of flowers on a plant was a sign of death, and to cut and bring them into the home invited bad luck.

One of the achievements of Le Nôtre, Louis XIV's landscape architect, was to introduce various herbaceous species into the gardens at Versailles and Fontainebleau. This firmly established it as a flower of importance.

As traditional superstitions started to die out, the peony became ever more widely grown. The work of French growers and hybridisers in the late nineteenth and early twentieth centuries was largely responsible for its prominent status in our gardens today.

The French breeders Crousse, Calot and Lemoine perfected the first scented herbaceous varieties, many of them raised from *P. officinalis* seedlings, which were known originally as peony roses. These were grown widely all over Europe and rivalled even the rose in popularity.

The development of the tree peony began in China around 700 AD and it quickly became a hallowed plant. During the Sung dynasty, between 960 and 1279, one species, *P. moutan*, was hailed unequivocally as the king of all flowers. Its blooms were depicted on ceramics and scholars dedicated entire treatises to it. In Chinese *moutan* means most beautiful and, at the height of its popularity, specimens were sold for a hundred ounces of gold. Since the fourteenth century *P. moutan* and *P. lutea* (now classified as *P. delavayi* var. *lutea*) have grown in the Imperial Gardens in Peking and, together with the herbaceous Chinese *P. lactiflora*, they are now found in gardens all over the world. *P. moutan* still grows in its original habitat in the Shantung province and Shanghai – today it is referred to as *P. suffruticosa*. In the fifteenth century the peony was carried from China to Samarkand and it is mentioned in contemporaneous Persian literature, but it was not until the eighteenth century that the tree peony was introduced to the Western world.

Before the 1800s there is surprisingly little evidence of either tree or herbaceous peony in America. Then, in the early nineteenth century, *Bartram's Garden Catalogue* was published. This list of foreign plants imported from abroad included a few tree peonies and herbaceous species such as *P. rosea* and *P. officinalis*.

Various societies were set up solely devoted to the study and breeding of peonies, and much of the best work on this notoriously difficult-to-breed flower is taking place today in North America. Klehm's of Illinois are the leaders in the field and continue to introduce new varieties. Poland is the only other country to have a firmly established development programme.

Owing to its longevity, the peony is very often an inherited plant, continuing to grow where originally planted, and it has proved the inspiration for many gardeners to expand and improve their collection.

The herbaceous peony has remained a firm favourite to this day. It ranges in colour from the purest single white cup, through feathery pinks, to the deepest double blowsiest red. With its many layers of perfume, from rose-scented to spicy clove, it is a visual and satisfactory feast.

The rather prosaically named American-bred 'Cheddar Cheese' is like a bowl of fluffy clotted cream. Another good variety is 'White Wings', a glorious large single yellowish-white cup-shaped flower. *P. mlokosewitschii*, from the Caucasus, bears large single cup-shaped cool lemon blooms, has a pinkish-bronze foliage and proffers a wondrous perfume. The foliage remains after the flowers are over and contributes useful colour within the border. In the home a lavish bowl of blooms is hard to surpass.

FLOWERING SEASON: They flower early in summer.
SOIL CONDITIONS: Easily grown in fertile soil that drains freely.
SITUATE: In the sun, but they will tolerate some shade.
PROPAGATION: Sow seed from species in pots in late autumn, but have patience. Divide herbaceous clumps either in spring or late autumn. Grafting of tree peonies is best left to specialists.
RESILIENCE: Hardy but tree peonies can be damaged by frost.
CARE: Shelter the young growth of tree peonies, as they are subject to mould. Eel worms can also be a problem. Prune tree peonies if they get out of shape.

PREVIOUS PAGE: Herbaceous peonies in shades of feathery pink have long been garden favourites.
OPPOSITE: The frilled fluffiness of *Paeonia* 'Cheddar Cheese' contrasts with the single white blooms of *P.* 'White Wings'.
BELOW: The deep red flowers of *P.* 'Charm' are right at the other end of the colour range.

Papaver (Papaveraceae)

poppy

Like gorgeous cancan girls, poppies dance in a garden, their tousled skirts held aloft, and smudged with pollen as black as kohl.

The field poppy, *Papaver rhoeas*, which grows wild in the British Isles, Europe and North Africa, was inseparable from corn in earlier times. Now considered a weed, it was once believed to ensure an abundant harvest. The poppy was named daughter of the field by the Assyrians and was sacred to both Aphrodite and the Roman goddess Ceres who, wearing a crown of wheat, held a blazing torch in one hand, and corn and poppies in the other. Figurines of poppy goddesses were placed in the temple at Knossos in Crete. Wearing what appear to be crinolines and crowned with large seedheads, they have an extraordinarily enigmatic presence. You can see them for yourself today in the Archaeological Museum in Heraklion.

After the battle of Waterloo in 1815 the ploughed fields were red with poppies, said to be the blood of the fallen. Again, they covered the fields of Flanders after the First World War and have ever since been the British flower of remembrance. Poppy seed needs light to germinate, and the ground churned by men in battle enabled their growth.

Smelling the field poppy was said to induce migraine, but it was also thought possible to cure headaches by drinking a decoction. The flowers are notoriously short-lived and have a

OPPOSITE: The sugary shades of *Papaver rhoeas* Shirley Series seem to glow in the sunlight.

habit of shedding their petals as soon as they are picked. Robert Burns wrote in 'Tam o Shanter' in 1791: 'But pleasures are like poppies spread, You seize the flow'r, its bloom shed.'

The field poppy, the symbol of remembrance, has been overshadowed by the opium poppy, *P. somniferum*, associated with oblivion and cultivated for centuries for its seed and sap. Remains have been discovered in Neolithic settlements and it is still farmed today to produce opium and its by-products. A native of Europe and Asia, it was perhaps introduced to Britain by the Romans, and by John Gerard's time in the sixteenth century there were several garden varieties, some double. Housewives made a tea from them, which was used particularly for rheumatism; it was also useful for calming fractious babies and as a sleeping draught. These poppies were grown in cottage gardens for medicinal properties rather than their beauty. The edible seeds were also used in cooking, and still are, as they have no soporific properties. Gerard noted that the seed 'is good to season bread with'.

The oriental poppy, *P. orientale*, a hardy perennial, arrived in Europe from south-west Asia in the early eighteenth century, followed by other closely related species. A magnificent show-stopper of a garden flower, with great sumptuous red flowers on hairy stems, it remained unchanged for nearly two centuries. Then in 1906, Amos Perry, a nurseryman from Enfield in Middlesex, noticed a pale pink seedling, which he developed. Seven years later a disgruntled customer complained of a white

poppy spoiling his pink-red border. From this lone specimen Amos Perry bred 'Perry's White', which is still cultivated today. He went on to turn his attention to shell pinks, deep reds and cerises with fringed edges, and developed the extensive range now available.

Another member of the family is the yellow horned poppy, *Glaucium flavum*, from Europe and the Mediterranean. Its habitat of shingle is a perfect foil for its sturdy green foliage and soft golden petals. Theophrastus recommended the root as a purgative and the leaves for treating sheep's ulcerated eyes. Dioscorides prescribed it for 'sciatica and liver griefs'.

In the late nineteenth century the Reverend Wilks of Shirley near Croydon created the Shirley poppies. These are offspring of *P. rhoeas*, the wild field poppy. He spotted one in a field near his house with petals edged in white. By marking the plant he was able to collect its seed when the flowers had finished, and breed a whole spectrum of poppies with coloured edges.

Poppies have a short but glorious flowering season in the garden, and are such bold inhabitants they cannot be ignored. They make excellent cutting flowers and last well if the freshly cut stems are plunged into boiling water before arranging. A vegetable garden gains a new dimension when planted with intermittent drifts of their wonderful delicate flowers. The tissue-paper flowers of *P. rhoeas*, which is a hardy annual, are perfect in an unkempt wild garden. Left to their own devices, they scatter themselves everywhere, emerging even from brick paths and the tops of walls.

FLOWERING SEASON: High summer.
SOIL CONDITIONS: Rich soil that drains freely.
SITUATE: In full sunshine.
PROPAGATION: Scatter seed of annuals in the garden in spring. Divide large clumps of perennials, again in the spring.
RESILIENCE: They are hardy, but some can be prone to frost.
CARE: Self-sufficient, but they can be affected by mildew.

The blowsy opium poppy, *P. somniferum*, another hardy annual, looks good in herb gardens. After flowering, its corn-coloured seedheads blend with sage and fennel to form a tapestry backdrop. There are both single and double varieties, in a vast range of colours.

The oriental poppy, *P. orientale*, a hardy perennial and a great big beauty, forms large clumps. Follow Gertrude Jekyll's advice and plant it with gypsophila. With her attention to detail, she devised this ruse so that the dying foliage is hidden as the gypsophila grows up around it. Or choose your own disguise for its untidy aftermath. Try *P. orientale* 'Beauty of Livermere', which has huge flowers of a wonderful deep red, or 'Black and White', which has great drama. In a pink border plant 'Juliane', with its beautiful fragile pale pink flowers. The large black stamens give it a startlingly exotic appearance. When the flowers are finished, the seedheads can be cut and dried for flower arrangements.

BELOW: *Papaver. orientalis* 'Patty's Plum' growing alongside alliums in a private garden in Suffolk, England.
OPPOSITE: *P. orientalis* 'Beauty of Livermere'.

Passiflora (Passifloraceae)

passion flower

Early Spanish missionaries to South America named the passion flower. They likened the blooms to the Passion of Christ, using their curious structure to represent different elements of the story. The ten petals and sepals symbolised the ten apostles – excluding Judas and Peter – while the corona within them represented the crown of thorns. The flower's five anthers stood for Christ's wounds, and the three stigmas the nails of the cross. Even the tendrils were supposedly reminiscent of the scourges and whips of Christ's tormentors.

Plants were brought to Europe at the beginning of the seventeenth century to great acclaim. Herbalist John Parkinson grew the first comer to Britain, namely *Passiflora incarnata*. *P. caerulea*, the common passion flower, a much easier species to grow, reached Britain at the end of the seventeenth century and is still widely grown. It bears blue flowers, although white varieties were also developed. They proved to be great favourites in Victorian gardens, as they are almost fully hardy if grown against a sheltered wall.

The delicious fruit of the passion flower is savoured worldwide. The purple passion fruit, *P. edulis* is grown commercially, as is *P. edulis flavicarpa*, and records show the fruit was being sold in Covent Garden Market, London, in 1914. The juice is delicious and the pulp is used to make jams and preserves. Just cutting open a wrinkled deep purple fruit and scooping out the seeds is a sensuous delight. Soaps, creams and bath oils made with passion-flower extract impart a luxurious tropical air to a bathroom.

The giant granadilla, *P. quadrangularis*, has melon-sized fruit, which can be used as a vegetable or eaten raw in fruit salad, and the pulp is used to make juice. In Brazil its rind is used to alleviate asthma, diarrhoea and insomnia.

The passion flower, of which there are more than four hundred varieties, is a native of the tropics, growing in North, South and Central America, as well as tropical Australasia and the islands of the Pacific.

The genus is the food plant of the caterpillars of the stunningly beautiful *Heliconiinae* butterflies, and passion flowers are often grown on butterfly farms.

Passion flowers will grow in a cool conservatory. Unfortunately the great hot-houses of the Victorian era have all but disappeared, so spectacular hanging canopies can not be seen in cooler climates. The moderately hardy species, such as *P. caerulea* and its cultivars, flourish in sheltered positions and, as summer seems to grow ever hotter, even produce fruit that ripens. They look glorious scrambling up trellises.

A great curtain of *P. coccinea* is an awesome sight in the tropical rainforest of Northern

Queensland in Australia, as its orange-scarlet flowers glow in the softly, filtered green light under the tree canopy. Now that many homes in cooler climates have a heated garden room or conservatory, it is possible to grow and enjoy some of the varieties that were previously only seen in warmer zones.

FLOWERING SEASON: From summer through to autumn.
SOIL CONDITIONS: Fairly rich soil that drains freely.
SITUATE: In sunshine, but they tolerate dappled shade.
PROPAGATION: Sow seed of species in spring. In autumn cuttings can be taken from established plants.
RESILIENCE: There are many tender species plus some moderately hardy ones.
CARE: Prune in spring. They can be affected by plant viruses.

PREVIOUS PAGE: The complex structure that gave the passion flower its name can be seen in the flowers of *Passiflora quadrangularis*.
BELOW: *P. coccinea* is not reliably hardy, but it can be grown in conservatories in temperate areas.
OPPOSITE: The delicate blooms of *P. foetida*

Phalaenopsis (Orchidaceae)

moth orchid

The flawless beauty of the exquisite moth orchid brings joy to the aesthete in us all. Phalaenopsis orchids are named after the Greek for moth, and when they sway in a light breeze you can immediately see why.

In their natural environment phalaenopsis plants grow on trees at a great height. They hail from forests in northern Australia, south-eastern Asia and even the Himalayas. Epiphytes or air plants, they live on trees, which they use for support, but are not parasitical.

In ideal conditions they are protected from the sun by the canopy of the rainforest, and drenched each day by tropical showers. They develop long and straggling root systems, which enable them to absorb moisture from the air.

A great many books have been written on the subject and cultivation of orchids, and societies dedicated to their cultivation have been founded worldwide. Anyone deciding to grow them will find others only too happy to share their passion.

The moth orchid is enjoying popularity as a house plant. Advances in cloning techniques have led to the commercialisation of orchid growing, so that saleable flowering plants can be produced in a matter of months rather than years. My favourite, *P. allegria*, is of the purest white, and is a supreme example, but other white varieties are readily available from many florists, as well as those of the most delicate pinks. These plants are very long-lived, and in today's centrally heated homes they are easy to keep, provided you mist them daily to mimic the high humidity of the rainforest. They can be bought as cut flowers but are more rewarding as house plants, living far longer and being a constant source of joy.

FLOWERING SEASON: They can flower for most of the year.
SOIL CONDITIONS: On a piece of bark or suspended in special compost.
SITUATE: In filtered light.
PROPAGATION: It is possible to take root cuttings.
RESILIENCE: Susceptible to frost.
CARE: Keep them in moist warm humid conditions.

ABOVE: The pure white flowers of *P.* 'Allegria' illustrate the beauty that has made the orchid an object of desire over the years.
OPPOSITE: *Phalaeonopsis* Ann Krull 'Zuma Canyon'.

Primula (Primulaceae)

candelabra primula

The luminescent tiered stems of candelabra primulas look their best beside running water or at the margins of a pond. Many are native to the Himalayas and eastern Asia, where they grow in bogs or, at the very least, damp and moisture-retentive soil.

Candelabra primulas form one of the three groups of primula, the other two being auriculas and polyanthus. They are robust herbaceous perennials and their common name alludes to the arrangements of their flowers, which are held on a tall stem and form several tiers.

Candelabra primulas are relatively recent arrivals, introduced some time around the 1920s. The summer-flowering *Primula wilsonii* var. *anisodora* is an enchanting example from the Yunnan province of China. Its sturdy stems emerge from large ruffs of leaves and bear tiers of deepest purple flowers with the soft smell of aniseed, as its name suggests.

Other varieties to be enjoyed are *P. beesiana*, which is a semi-evergreen species from the damp meadows of the mountains of south-west China. It is hardy and has many tiers of yellow-centred saucer-shaped flowers of a deep pink. *P. chungensis*, from China and Bhutan, has soft orange flowers, again saucer-shaped, produced in early summer and sweetly fragrant. *P.* 'Inverewe' is of the brightest red, produces many stems and makes an impressive addition to the garden; it blooms in summer.

Few of us have streams, bogs or lakes in our gardens, but the edge of even a small pond benefits from their inclusion. Laying a sheet of heavy-duty polythene a foot or so below the soil's surface to slow up drainage can help establish a bog garden if you keep it well-watered.

FLOWERING SEASON: From the onset of spring to summer.
SOIL CONDITIONS: Damp rich soil.
SITUATE: They like to be shaded.
PROPAGATION: Scatter seed at the beginning of spring. Divide clumps during winter.
RESILIENCE: Pleasingly hardy.
CARE: Self-sufficient, but they need moisture.

OPPOSITE: The painted blooms of *Primula beesiana* seem to glow with an inner light.

Primula veris (Primulaceae)

cowslip

The demure cowslip bows its head in newly green meadows, whispering that spring is here. The cowslip is native to Britain and acquired its name from the old English cu-slyppe, which has two interpretations. One is cow pat or dung, because the plants flourish in meadows and were thought to grow from the ground that cows had manured. Another translation of cu-slyppe is the breath of cows, from cow's lips. I prefer the latter, for when milking Daisy, my almond-eyed Jersey cow, the smell of her breath was of sweet summer meadows. That still time of day at dawn and dusk in the milking parlour is one of my most poignant memories, and dear Daisy was certainly kept in meadows strewn with cowslips. There is a northern European legend that likens the cowslip to a bunch of keys. St Peter was said to have dropped his keys to heaven on hearing that another set existed, and the cowslip sprang from the ground where they fell.

John Gerard grew cowslips and had double varieties in his garden in the sixteenth century. The cowslip was also known as palsywort at this time, perhaps from sympathetic magic that likened the illness to the plants' trembling flowers. One reference in a fifteenth-century manuscript seems to support this theory, as it recommended boiling cowslips and lavender in ale, to be drunk as a cure for trembling hands.

In years gone by bunches of the flowers were made into balls, which were tossed in the air to the familiar incantation: 'Tinker, tailor, soldier, sailor, rich man, poor man, beggar man, thief'. Girls anxious to know their future husband's trade tossed them and let them fall to the ground, each probably hoping for the 'tossty-mossty' or 'tisty-tosty' to land on 'rich man'.

For centuries the flowers have been used to produce the most prized of homemade wines. Unless you have your own personal cowslip meadow, there's no chance of gathering enough flowers to make wine these days.

In the mid-seventeenth century cowslips were strongly recommended for inclusion in wild-meadow gardens, in the company of sweet violets and wild strawberries. There is renewed interest in this style of planting.

Cowslips thrive on grassland, and are easily introduced into orchards and on banks alongside streams. Seeds and plants are widely available and, once established, spread with ease. To walk in the garden in spring and see the first soft green leaves appear lifts the heart; a sure sign of the death of winter and the promise of things to come. Longer evenings, soft misty mornings – all yearned for after the long drawn-in nights of winter. As Milton wrote in *Comus* in 1637:

> *'Thus I set my printless feet*
> *O'er the cowslip's velvet head*
> *That bends not as I tread.'*

FLOWERING SEASON: Throughout spring.
SOIL CONDITIONS: Fairly rich soil that drains freely.
SITUATE: They are happiest in sunlight, but will tolerate some shade.
PROPAGATION: Seed can be scattered in the garden in spring. Clumps can be divided during winter.
RESILIENCE: Hardy.
CARE: Self-sufficient.

OPPOSITE: The unpretentious charm of the cowslip deserves to be appreciated in its own right.

Ranunculus (Ranunculaceae)

ranunculus

The golden buttercup that shines in ancient pastures throughout Britain is one of the most uplifting sights of summer. Since time immemorial small children have held these lustrous flowers under their chins to see if they like butter. And since the flowers without fail cast a golden glow on the skin, the answer is always yes. Rubbed on cows' udders, the flowers were said to improve the cow's milk and yield, but the effect was rather hard to evaluate, for they would have brushed against them anyway, as they grazed.

The Latin name, in use since Pliny's day, comes from *rana* or frog, maybe because the plants thrive in damp conditions. All the native species have double forms, which were referred to by John Gerard in the sixteenth century as bachelor's buttons. The double-flowered *Ranunculus aconitifolius* or Fair Maids of France has virtually disappeared from today's gardens, yet was enormously popular then. The sixteenth century brought a host of flowers to Europe, and gardens were transformed. Before this period most plants were grown simply for their medicinal properties.

Sir John Chardin, travelling in Persia in the 1660s, described the native flowers he saw in his travel notes. He tells of fields with wild single red ranunculas, tulips, anemones and crown imperials – all likely inhabitants of the paradise gardens of that time.

By the late seventeenth century ranunculas were being developed by keen landowners, who were the forerunners of the humbler flower societies. *R. asiaticus* was raised by René Morin, an eminent Parisian nurseryman. The species was taken up with enthusiasm by the emerging societies, and by the end of the eighteenth century ranunculas almost rivalled the tulip in popularity. They were available in colours from white to red, brown to violet, purple to crimson, striped and spotted.

By the late eighteenth century there were 800 forms to choose from, yet by the end of the century the choices were few. Many proved difficult to cultivate, which probably explains their fall from grace.

In their native habitat – from Asia to north Africa, Europe, North America and New Zealand – a field of these delicate beauties is entrancing. From white, blushed with the palest pink, to deep pink blushed with purple, they sway gracefully in the breeze, their centres smudged with black.

I fill our little stone house in Crete with great bunches of them – gathering wildflowers is a national pursuit on these richly clad hillsides. The flowers last for days, shedding the odd soft petal, and I can selfishly enjoy their all-too-brief flowering season.

In the gardens of the Southern Highlands in Australia *R. asiaticus* thrives in profusion, creating a wonderful background in borders and filling gaps in a breathtaking way. The flowers seem so exotic to someone used to the gardens of the northern hemisphere. The white blooms look like inverted ballerinas and have a simple purity and softness, while the choice of other colours spans the spectrum – for me, the dark browns are the most exotic.

FLOWERING SEASON: They flower at the beginning of summer.
SOIL CONDITIONS: Very rich damp soil that drains freely.
SITUATE: In full sunshine, but they will tolerate shade.
PROPAGATION: Sow ripe seed under glass. Tubers can be divided in both spring and autumn.
RESILIENCE: Hardy, except for *R. asiaticus.*
CARE: They are self-sufficient in the right conditions.

RIGHT: *Ranunculus* 'Rembrandt'.
OVERLEAF: It is easy to see why ranunculus make popular cut flowers: when massed together, their many-petalled rosettes have a sumptuous air.

Rosa (Rosaceae)

rose

The rose is the undisputed queen of the garden. Deep dark reds, black within their depths; pristine delicate white bowls of scented bliss; soft tumbling pink feathery balls, clambering through trees and trellises – the flowers are sublime. In autumn they bead the bushes with glowing fruit, which last well into winter.

The rose's beauty, perfume and healing properties have been known since the beginning of time. Bunches of roses were found in the tomb of Tutankhamun, having survived for 30 centuries. The walls of the Minoan Palace at Knossos in Crete have frescoes of roses.

In Ancient Rome important guests were showered with rose petals and their mattresses filled with them. Roses were also used medicinally. Pliny advocated the rose gall – a reddish-yellow ball formed by the egg of the gall wasp – as a cure-all. Known as bedeguars, these briar balls were sold by apothecaries as a diuretic, to disperse kidney stones, for colic and as a vermifuge. Ground and mixed with honey they were used as a hair restorer. They were also used as amulets to ward off whooping cough.

Rose-petal infusions were said to alleviate rheumatism, cure acne and soothe sore eyes. Arab doctors used rose jelly for the treatment of tuberculosis, as did apothecaries in the Middle Ages. Until quite recently rose-hip syrup was given to babies as a source of vitamin C.

LEFT: An arrangement of Rosa 'Golden Celebration' and 'Golden Wing' presents exquisite subtleties in colouring.
OPPOSITE: A sugar-pink rose looks almost edible.

The rose is unsurpassed in the perfume industry. Avicenna, an Arabian doctor who lived at the end of the tenth century, was the first to distil perfume from roses. It takes 125kg (250lbs) of petals to produce 25g (1oz) of attar of roses. Around Kazanluk in Turkey, the land is literally carpeted with pink roses, and thousands of tons are produced each year for the perfume industry. Morocco also grows vast fields of roses, as does Grasse in France.

Medieval monastic gardens produced flowers for nosegays and garlands for church festivals, the main ingredient being roses. During the sixteenth century the more enlightened provided bowls of rosewater in guests' bedrooms and rosewater was sprinkled on clothes and floors. Housekeepers made sachets that were placed among clothes, and also pot-pourri, to freshen the rooms (which was advisable in those somewhat pungent times).

Ancient roses are still in cultivation today and centuries-old species are readily available. *R. gallica* was introduced to Britain by the Romans. *R. damascena* was brought back by the Crusaders. Gerard wrote of *R. spinosissima*, the Burnet or Scots rose, growing in the village of Knightsbridge. Of all flowers, roses most lend themselves to photography with grace, their velvet depths seemingly redolent with perfume even in the pages of a book. David Austin's English roses are for me a prolific source of inspiration. Each year more new varieties are developed that have the charm of old-fashioned roses but with the added advantage of a continuous flowering season, which in a small garden is an extremely useful quality.

To choose roses for your gardens it is best to go to a specialist nursery, where they can be seen growing and expert advice is dispensed freely. There is a shape and size for any situation in a garden, courtyard or even windowbox. A well-chosen mix can supply a summer-long flowering season, and few things surpass the joy of cutting roses to bring into the house. Great bunches of roses, their petals dropping on to darkly polished wood, the scent pervading the air with its sweetness, is one of my supreme joys in life.

FLOWERING SEASON: From the middle of summer to its end.
SOIL CONDITIONS: Fairly rich soil that drains freely.
SITUATE: In sunshine, but they are tolerant of some shade.
PROPAGATION: Best planted at the beginning of winter.
RESILIENCE: Most are fully hardy though some can be susceptible to frost.
CARE: Prune at the beginning of either winter or spring. They need feeding, and a mulch helps them through the winter.

OPPOSITE: A display of *Rosa* 'Heather Austin' and *R.* 'Constance Spry' has all the qualities of a still-life.

Rudbeckia (Asteraceae)

black-eyed susan

The jaunty yellow saucers of rudbeckia, with those contrasting dark eyes that give them their common name, animate the garden with simple appeal. These native North American plants were named by Linnaeus in honour of Olof Rudbeck Junior, a tutor at the University of Uppsala in Sweden. Linnaeus was tutor to his three youngest children (he produced 24), the appointment rescuing him from poverty. Both Rudbeck Junior and his father were also leading botanists of their time.

Rudbeckias grow in light woodlands and meadows, shining on roadsides and glowing in sunlit glades. They are best grown as annuals, although many species are actually short-lived perennials, and are ideal for filling in those inevitable gaps in borders. The tall stems hold solitary daisy-like flowers at their tip. *Rudbeckia hirta*, meaning hairy, has many cultivars, ranging in colour from the palest golden yellow to deepest bronze.

Naturalised in woodland, they look almost indigenous and they also make good tall ingredients in a wildflower meadow. A large swathe of garden given over to annuals of all types, including rudbeckias, planted in a seemingly random manner is a wonderful spectacle. Glorious clashing colours, apparently unplanned, sing forth. Rudbeckias are also valuable as long-lasting cut flowers, and bring sunshine into the home.

FLOWERING SEASON: Throughout summer into autumn.
SOIL CONDITIONS: Fairly rich soil that drains freely.
SITUATE: They enjoy sunshine, but tolerate some shade.
PROPAGATION: Sow seed under glass in spring. Clumps can be divided in both autumn and spring.
RESILIENCE: Hardy.
CARE: Self-sufficient, but they enjoy moisture.

OPPOSITE: The bright flowers of rudbeckia make them impossible to ignore in a garden.

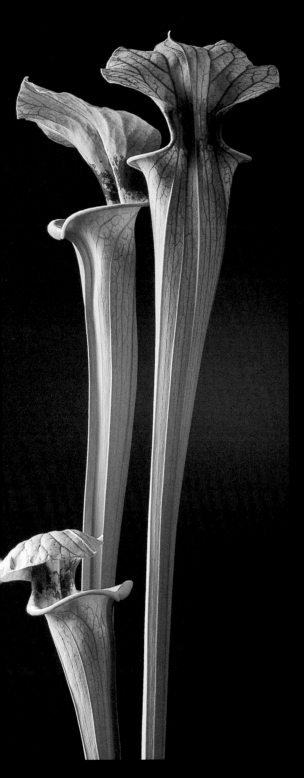

Sarracenia (Sarraceniaceae)
pitcher plant

The bewitching flowers of the sarracenia, held resplendently above the ominous pitchers that lurk beneath, are almost orchid-like in their beauty. They are for me one of nature's triumphant oddities.

The sarracenia is an insectivorous genus, whose common name is pitcher plant: self-explanatory, as its trumpets resemble pitchers. It is found from the Arctic regions of Canada to areas around New York in the USA, and even as far south as Florida, where it lives in bogs and poor soil. It was brought to Europe, and the species *S. purpurea* or huntman's cup has since become naturalised in bogs in Switzerland and Ireland. The sarracenia was introduced into Britain by John Tradescant the Younger in about 1640, but went unnamed until the eighteenth century, when it acquired the name sarracenia after the Canadian botanist and physician Dr M. Sarrazin de l'Etang.

For me, insectivorous plants have a slightly sinister quality. Seemingly innocent, they sit waiting for some hapless creature to be beguiled by their beauty and nectar, only to slip down the pitcher to its death. Sentimentality aside, the pitcher plant is indeed a beguiling plant in all ways. The genus has eight species of perennials, whose colours range from cream and yellow to the darkest red, with flowers borne aloft on long straight stems above the pitchers.

Sarracenia are much in demand, which has led to the plunder of their natural habitat. Coupled with land drainage and development schemes, this has put several species at risk, and some are nearly extinct. The devastation of this and other plants in the wild makes the national collections held in Britain invaluable. Dedicated growers care for and propagate endangered plants, and make them once again available to all in an ecologically friendly manner. Luckily sarracenia have benefited from this scheme.

Expert growers recommend hardy varieties such as *S. purpurea*, with its pitchers of green and purple, surmounted by purple, pink, red or sometimes even yellow flowers. *S. flava* has pure soft yellow flowers and tall pitchers. Although rare in the wild, it is available through nurseries and makes a good house plant. Hardy varieties are spectacular planted in boggy moist areas in the garden, while as a houseplant not only are they exotic to look at, they are very discreet fly-killers, altogether preferable to an insecticide spray.

FLOWERING SEASON: They flower mostly in the spring.
SOIL CONDITIONS: Rich damp soil that contains no lime.
SITUATE: Indoors they like to be protected from full sunlight. Outdoors they enjoy the sun.
PROPAGATION: Sown in spring, the seed tray should be placed in water, again with no lime content. They can be transplanted after the tiny pitchers emerge.
RESILIENCE: Most are hardy, but they can be prone to frost.
CARE: Keep moist with water that contains no lime. Indoors they need feeding and it is a good idea to stand pots in a shallow dish of water, again with no lime content.

LEFT: *Sarracenia* x Brooks Hybrid.
OPPOSITE: The beautiful flowers of *S. 'Judy' minor* x *excellens* are held above its slender trumpets on long stalks.

Scabiosa (Dipsacaceae)

scabious

The scabious is a plant of open fields and grassy banks throughout temperate Europe and Asia. In the days when wildflowers could be gathered with impunity, many a small pudgy hand bore a bunch triumphantly home. Known commonly as either the mourning bride or the pincushion flower, it blooms throughout the summer months.

Long before medieval times, the scabious was held invaluable for treating skin eruptions and scabies, hence its name. The species grown in medieval gardens would probably have been *Scabiosa columbaria*, the delicate blue wildflower. The juice from the stem was said to act against the plague and to be an antidote to snake-bites.

The genus includes about 90 species, which encompass annuals, biennials and perennials, and colours ranging from white, through pinks and blues, to deepest purple.

Herbalist John Gerard grew scabious in 1597 and described 17 types; he advised using it against pestilent fevers. John Parkinson described and grew *S. atropurpurea*, the annual scabious from the south of Europe. It has deeply fragrant flowers that are purply-red.

By the eighteenth century the colours available included pinks and purples. These subtle gradations of hue are invaluable to use almost as a colourwash, linking whites to pinks to blues in the garden. Choose examples from the part of the spectrum that works for you and your garden. The plant itself is useful as it helps to disguise fading spring foliage that dies untidily. *S. caucasia* is the variety most commonly grown now. It has pale blue flowers and arrived from the Caucasus at the beginning of the nineteenth century.

Both annuals and perennials provide bedding plants and are of great value in mixed planting. The beautiful disc-shaped flowers nod atop almost leafless stems, and if dead-headed will go on and on. They attract bees and butterflies and make enchanting additions to a wild garden or flowering meadow.

As a cut flower the scabious is long-lasting, and its shape makes a good punctuation mark in a large arrangement. As an added bonus, the dried seedheads look good as well.

FLOWERING SEASON: Throughout the summer months.
SOIL CONDITIONS: They prefer chalky soil that drains freely.
SITUATE: They are sun-loving but will tolerate some shade.
PROPAGATION: Sow seed of annuals and biennials at the beginning of spring in the required site. Perennials are best sown under glass at the same time. Large clumps can be divided again at the same time, refreshing the soil every few years.
RESILIENCE: Mostly hardy.
CARE: Self-sufficient.

OPPOSITE: *Scabiosa gigantea* (syn. *Cephalaria gigantea*).

Strelitzia (Strelitziaceae)

bird of paradise flower

The bizarrely outrageous bird of paradise flower lives up to its name. Like some great beaked denizen of the forest, it seems poised, ready to soar off at the slightest provocation. These extremely handsome plants are natives of South Africa: there are five species that grow on the banks of rivers and clearings in the bush. Botanically they were named after Queen Charlotte Sophia, Duchess of Mecklenberg-Strelitz and wife of King George III of England.

The striking flowers are very long-lasting, and therefore invaluable in the cut-flower trade. The plants can grow to enormous heights, with dark green glossy paddle-shaped leaves and the bird-like flowers towering above head height. I encountered them in all their glory in tropical Northern Queensland in Australia, where they are grown in the company of heliconias and ginger lilies for the cut-flower market.

The growers rise at 4am to cut these extravagant blooms, before the steamy heat of the day. Walking through this primeval landscape under the rain canopy was the experience of a lifetime. The forest never sleeps, and resounds with the most extraordinary cries. Tree pythons, leeches and unseen creatures lurk everywhere. Yet the flowers triumph over fear.

If these strange, magnificent plants can be grown outside, they introduce an outstanding elemental air to a garden, but they must not encounter frost at all. For those of us in colder climes, they thrive in a greenhouse and look fabulous mixed with large succulents. If you lack a greenhouse large enough for them, be content to buy them from the florist. Take the flowers home and imagine the eerie cries that surround them in the rainforest glades of Northern Queensland, perhaps a little grateful that there are no deadly creatures to be braved. It is possible to grow them outside in cooler climes you sometimes see them growing on roundabouts in London as a summer bedding – but they must be protected or brought indoors in winter if they are to survive.

FLOWERING SEASON: They flower in winter through to spring.
SOIL CONDITIONS: Rich damp soil that drains freely.
SITUATE: They need plenty of light but some shade from direct sun.
PROPAGATION: Sow seed in containers in a greenhouse, but they are very slow to mature. In large pots, plants need compost that contains loam. They can be moved outside once frosts have ended.
RESILIENCE: They are susceptible to frost.
CARE: They are self-sufficient outdoors, but require feeding inside.

BELOW: Against a contrasting background, it becomes obvious how the bird of paradise flower came by its common name.
OPPOSITE: *Strelitzia reginae*, also known as the crane flower, growing in a private garden in California.

Jade has been highly prized and collected for centuries. This opulent vine mirrors the precious stone's elusive quality and colour, and is aptly named. The great pendulous bunches of flowers are ever astir, with an unforgettable intensity of colour. As to its Latin name, a strongyle is a parasitic worm, so perhaps *Strongylodon* refers to the way the vine climbs over its neighbours; *macrobotrys* is a reference to its huge hanging clusters of flowers.

Florida is a major tourist destination that has hidden gems such as the Fairchild Botanical Gardens in Coral Gables, Miami. A long pergola hugs a wall and is festooned with the unbelievable hanging blossoms – or racemes – of the jade vine. They are like gigantic, translucent-green talons, which seem to tremble with movement, even on the stillest day. The vine has an eerie quality and the colour is so extraordinary it seems not of this world.

Jade vines also grow in the newly restored Palm House in London's Kew Gardens. To enter this wonderful humid glasshouse is the closest most Britons come to a tropical forest, and the atmosphere is magical. Hot-houses are ideal to visit when there is a cold snap in the air – you can almost imagine that you have been transported to a jungle paradise. It must be the most incredible sight to see the jade vine flowering in its native habitat in the Philippines, but until I get the opportunity to do so, I shall continue to visit Kew.

FLOWERING SEASON: Winter to summer.
SOIL CONDITIONS: Fertile humus rich neutral to acid soil.
SITUATE: Full sun or partial shade.
PROPAGATION: Sow seed as soon as ripe. Root stem sections in summer
RESILIENCE: Frost-tender
CARE: Support prune after flowering. Indoors, water freely with growth. Apply liquid fertiliser every 2-3 weeks.

RIGHT AND OPPOSITE: *Strongylodon macrobotrys* grows in profusion in the Fairchild Botanical gardens in Florida.

Strongylodon (Leguminosae)

jade vine

Swainsona formosa (Papilionaceae)

Sturt's desert pea

The glowing flowers of the tenacious desert pea are like little bursts of flame, enlivening the land with their exuberant colour. The state emblem for South Australia, Sturt's desert pea was discovered on Rosemary Island in the Dampier Archipelago in 1699 by William Dampier, who described it as 'a creeping vine that runs along the ground, the blossom like a bean blossom, but much larger and of a deep red colour looking very beautiful'. He collected specimens which are housed in the herbarium at Oxford University.

Captain Charles Sturt recorded the plant in 1845 in the Australian hinterland 'towards Coopers Creek'. His journal, *Narrative of an Expedition into Central Australia*, refers to its beauty and the harsh environment it inhabits.

The genus *Swainsona* is named in honour of Isaac Swainson, who cultivated a private botanical garden in Twickenham near London in the late eighteenth century. *Swainsona formosa* was introduced into England in 1855. It failed to thrive on its own roots, but when grafted it was able to be grown as a spectacular flower in a hanging basket.

To the Aborigines the desert pea is a flower of blood. The Dream Time, tales handed down for aeons, include the story of a beautiful young girl, Purlimil, who fell in love with a handsome young man, Borola. They wished to marry, but the tribal elders had chosen Tirlta for Purlimil's husband. She protested, crying that he was old and angry. Borola and Purlimil could see no option but flight. Waiting for nightfall, they left, journeying to the shores of a beautiful lake where Borola's relations dwelt. They married and lived happily together for many seasons.

But Tirlta had not forgotten Purlimil. Hearing news of her from some nomadic hunters, he gathered together members of the tribe known for their cruelty. Attacking the camp at night, they killed everyone leaving a battlefield drenched in blood. The ancestral spirits, watching from the sky world, were so distressed by this slaughter of blameless people that they cried for days, so that the lakes became salty. Tirlta returned to the scene of destruction to gloat but there were no bodies to be seen, just a sea of beautiful flowers of the brightest scarlet. Stricken with fear, Tirlta turned to run away,

only to be hit by a spirit spear, by which he was instantly slain. His body was changed into a pebble where he fell.

In its natural harsh habitat the desert pea grows for only one season, often after rain. The flowers are usually red, but white-pink and pure green forms have been recorded. This stunning plant, with flowers gleaming at intervals along its soft grey creeping foliage, is an arresting sight. Sturt's desert pea is a difficult plant to cultivate from seed, but thrives on grafted rootstock, growing almost anywhere in Australia. It is particularly successful in large containers. I have even seen it growing in the smokestack of an old steam engine in New South Wales, glowing against the rusty metal.

FLOWERING SEASON: They flower from the onset of spring through to summer.
SOIL CONDITIONS: Fairly rich soil that drains freely.
SITUATE: In full sun
PROPAGATION: In spring sow seed that has been soaked. Root cuttings can be taken in summer.
RESILIENCE: They are susceptible to frost.
CARE: They are thirsty but self-sufficient.

OPPOSITE: The blood-red flowers of the desert pea are the stuff of Aboriginal legend.

Telopea speciosissima (Proteaceae)

waratah

The waratah deserves its importance in the folk-lore of aboriginal Australians. Closely observed, it possesses perfect order; viewed from afar, its bright red flower punctuates the bush with almost incandescent spots of colour.

The plant has been the official floral emblem of New South Wales since 1962 and has retained its aboriginal name, which was adopted by early settlers in the Port Jackson area. The botanical name *Telopea* comes from the Greek *telepos*, meaning seen from afar, as its brilliant flowers are visible in the bush from some distance away: *speciosissima* signifies very beautiful or handsome. Writing of the waratah in 1793, Sir James Smith, founder of the Linnaean Society in England, states: 'The most magnificent plant, which the prolific soil of New Holland affords is, by common consent, both of Europeans and natives, the Waratah. It is moreover a favourite with the latter, upon account of a rich honeyed juice which they sip from its flowers.'

One tale of how the waratah came to be comes from the aboriginal Dream Time. A newly initiated warrior, Bahmai, went on his first raiding expedition. He was watched from afar by Krubi, a young woman of his tribe who had long loved him. She waited for his return, knowing he would be attracted by her wallaby-skin cloak adorned with red feathers and be sure to claim her for his wife. As the shadows length-ened the warriors returned, but Bahmai was not among them. Krubi sank to the ground weeping., her tears forming a small stream. As it flowed down the valley, grass grew and flowers sprang to life. After seven days Krubi sank into the ground to join her lover, but the tiny rivulet continued to flow. Slowly a tender unknown shoot emerged. Its leaves were red-tipped, as Brahmai's spear had been, and its flowers were as red as the parrot's feathers on Krubi's cloak. So the waratah was born, a symbol of undying love.

There are four species in Eastern Australia. Protected in the wild, bush-rangers daub them with paint to deter thieves. The plants are so resilient that they can even survive bushfire by regenerating.

Long-lasting cut flowers, waratahs are grown north of Sydney and in Hawaii, New Zealand and Israel for this purpose. They have been introduced to Britain but cannot survive the winter and seldom flower, even in a glasshouse.

FLOWERING SEASON: They flower from spring through to summer.
SOIL CONDITIONS: Slightly acidic soil that drains freely. Indoors mix sand with compost that has a loam base.
SITUATE: They enjoy full sunlight, but will tolerate some shade.
PROPAGATION: Seed should be sown in pots under glass when ripe.
RESILIENCE: They do not tolerate frost.
CARE: They need plenty of water. They can be pruned when they have flowered.

RIGHT: The tightly packed flowerheads of the waratah are just as impressive when seen from afar.

Tulipus (*Liliaceae*)

tulip

The tulip is so named because of its resemblance to a turban, *tülbend* in Turkish. It was introduced to the West from Persia by Ogier Ghiselin de Busbecq, the Holy Roman Ambassador of Ferdinand I at the court of Suleiman the Magnificent. He sent seeds and bulbs back to Vienna in 1554 and the adoration of the tulip began.

It was first seen flowering in 1559 in a garden in Augsburg, which belonged to Councillor Harwart, a famous collector of rare bulbs. He had been sent them by a friend in Constantinople. Then in about 1562 a cargo of bulbs reached Antwerp , where some were eaten in error, but others survived and were grown. During the next decade the tulip became much sought after by wealthy Dutch and Germans. It arrived in Britain in 1577 or 1578, according to the herbalist John Gerard, who knew it as tulipa or Dalmatian cap. He said that the bulbs preserved in sugar were rather nourishing.

The desire to grow tulips spread to the middle classes. Including them in the garden showed one to be an arbiter of taste and style – it was, indeed, social suicide to be without them. But nothing in the entire history of cultivation can compare with the 'tulipomania' that swept through Holland in 1634. People began to pay unbelievable prices. One trader in Haarlem paid half of his entire fortune for a single bulb.

The striped tulip became the most covetable, though Parkinson noticed that these plants were weaker. It has only recently been understood that this striping or feathering was actually caused by a virus spread by aphids.

The ordinary business of Holland was neglected as all strata of society were caught up in tulipomania. The most desirable variety, 'Semper Augustus', could command a price of 5,500 florins, and at one point only two of these bulbs were available. One was purchased for 12 acres of building land, the other for 4,600 florins, plus a new carriage and pair, and a complete set of harness.

A wealthy merchant expected to acquire a very rare bulb in a consignment of cargo from the Levant. Looking for his precious bulb to no avail, the merchant sent out a search party to the docks, where the hapless captain of the ship was found eating the last of his 'onion'. The price of his breakfast would have supported an entire ship's crew for a year. Ignorance was no protection and he spent several months in prison, charged with theft.

An English amateur botanist who dissected a bulb he found in a conservatory was dragged through the streets, to the magistrate by the Dutch owner. The Englishman was told he owed 4,000 florins and was imprisoned until he had honoured his debt.

Prices fluctuated and dealers made colossal profits playing the market. People sold all in their quest for riches. Small towns threw vast banquets in taverns, which were used as 'showplaces', with large vases of tulips on display on all sides. Yet the mania was not to last, and the demise of the market was swift, reducing people from all walks of life to penury.

Dutch tulipomania was mirrored in England and France, but on a much smaller scale.

Eventually the once lionised tulip began to regain its status and value, so that, in 1800, a bulb in the catalogue of a London nursery was labelled at £200.

The fascinating history of the tulip began a new chapter with the foundation of the Wakefield and North of England Tulip Society in 1836, which still flourishes today. It is one of the original flower societies formed mainly by working-class men, who met to discuss and display their carefully nurtured blooms. The treasured old varieties are still exhibited in beer bottles at their annual flower show.

The passionate and intrepid plant collectors who roamed far and wide in the late nineteenth century supplied the flower societies with many

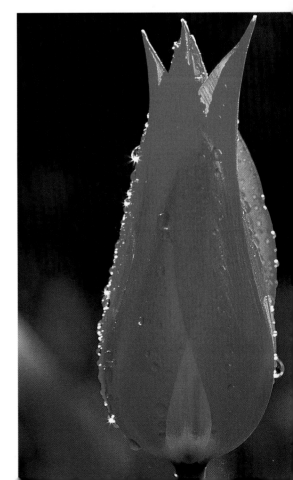

more species from lands as far away as Samarkand. Most of these still grow in their native habitats. *Tulipa lanata* was found in 1884 in Persia, and blooming on the roofs of mosques in Kashmir.

Tulips are indispensable in a spring garden to take over from the earlier daffodils, and are available in countless colours, sizes and forms. The single and double early tulips grow well in pots indoors and can be forced into bloom in mid winter. Planted in windowboxes they bring welcome splashes of colour to drab city streets.

The double varieties are long-lasting in the garden and have a sweet smell.

Short-stemmed cottage tulips are ideal for naturalising in flowery meads, but need to be tracked down, for they have been ousted by more modern varieties. Luscious parrot tulips, with their intense colours, certainly live up to their name and are sensational massed in ranks in a garden.

Meanwhile the search continues for the goal that eluded the seventeenth-century tulip breeder – the mythical black tulip.

FLOWERING SEASON: Throughout spring.
SOIL CONDITIONS: Rich soil that drains freely.
SITUATE: In sunlight, though they will tolerate some shade.
PROPAGATION: Bulbs should be planted at the end of summer. Seeds are extremely slow to mature.
RESILIENCE: They are obligingly hardy.
CARE: Self-sufficient, but in a small garden bulbs can be lifted and stored when they have finished flowering. Watch out for slugs.

ABOVE: Tulips and forget-me-nots (*Mysotis*) make a classic combination for a country-garden border.
OPPOSITE: Sunlight sparkles on a dew-covered bloom.
OVERLEAF: Vanilla petals are lavishly veined with brushstokes of strawberry red.

Verbascum (Scrophulariaceae)

mullein

The ancient mullein is a magical plant, steeped in myth and legend. It towers in the landscape, each magnificent spire leading the eye upwards. Mullein is also known as Aaron's rod, which, according to the Bible, 'was budded, and brought forth buds and bloomed blossoms'. It is widespread throughout the northern hemisphere, growing on roadsides and sunny banks. In the Mediterranean it towers magnificently above brooms, gorse, sages and euphorbias. Nature's own planting scheme is hard to surpass.

The mullein, from the Latin *mollis* or soft, which refers to its heavy leaves, has many local names: Our Lord's flannel, Moses' blanket, Virgin Mary's candle; and also hag taper and devil's blanket – indicating associations with both good and evil.

Mercury was said to have given a mullein plant to Ulysses to protect him from Circe's spells. In the first century AD Dioscorides suggested figs would ripen if placed with the leaves. The long-stemmed *Verbascum thapsus* has been dipped in tallow and used as a torch since Roman times. It is a giant of a plant, with soothing virtues. The golden flowers and leaves were powdered and inhaled to clear the nose.

The hag taper is described in John Gerard's *Herball* (stating that they grow 'on Black Heath next to London') along with the dark-leaved *V. nigrum* and the yellow-flowered *V. blattaria*, of which there was a white-flowered variety by the seventeenth century. The purple *V. phoeniceum*, from southern Europe and central Asia, was growing in Britain in the late sixteenth century and is the forebear of today's hybrids.

These species still grow here, but are rare. More usual are the yellow-flowered *V. chaixii*, introduced in the early nineteenth century from Europe. There is a white form, *V. chaixii* 'Album', which has purple centres to its flowers.

Verbascum is a genus of some 350 species, mostly biennial, with soft hairy leaves. Some are semi-evergreen, these being grown as much for their woolly foliage as for their flowers. Although the majority have yellow flowers, they can also be white, purple, red and brownish-red. 'Helen Johnson' has soft almost brown flowers that can make useful garden plants, for they are also not too tall.

In the eighteenth century 'bouquet garden' sunflowers were often the main feature, but in a modern reinterpretation verbascums would mix well, rivalling them in stature. They could be surrounded with plants of complementary colours and sizes, to create a lavish bed that still need not take up too much space. *V. olympicum*, with its golden-yellow candelabra, is a giant of a plant, and partnered with *V. phoeniceum*, with white to dark purple flowers, will add a vertical dimension to any border.

A wildflower garden could be enlivened by

FLOWERING SEASON: From midsummer to its close.
SOIL CONDITIONS: Poor soil that drains freely.
SITUATE: In the full sunshine they glory in.
PROPAGATION: Seed should be sown in pots at the end of spring under glass. Divide large clumps in spring.
RESILIENCE: They are mostly hardy.
CARE: Self-sufficient but the giants may need staking.

V. thapsus, although it, too, is tall. Self-introduced, wild mulleins flourished on my kitchen garden wall in Norfolk, glowing like large golden candles. As we increasingly have to consider gardening with less rainfall, these robust plants are obviously ideal, thrusting happily through gravel and requiring no attention to survive.

The modern hybrid verbascums come in all colours, shapes and sizes. Carefully chosen, there is an appropriate variety for almost every spot in the garden, I have mixed V. chaxii 'Album' with white foxgloves in vast urns, delighting in their great white luminescent spires in the garden at night, reflecting the glow from inside the house.

ABOVE: A successful white planting mixes violas and roses with V. chaixii 'Album'.
LEFT: Verbascum thapsus has velvety flowerbuds from which buttercup-yellow flowers burst forth.

Viola (Violaceae)

pansy

The violet, *Viola odorata*, forerunner of today's popular violas and pansies, is an ancient plant known throughout Europe, Asia and North Africa. Centuries ago it was the emblem of Athens, and was cultivated not only for the flower market but for its purple dye and for numerous medicinal remedies, as Theophrastus noted in about 320 BC.

The Arabs used violets to make sherbet, and in the Middle Ages the candied flowers were in great demand as sweetmeats. Today preserved violets are still used as cake decorations or to flavour fondant sweets.

Violets were grown commercially for many years for their use in the perfume industry, and also as cut flowers, but the two great wars more or less put paid to the crop. The invention of synthetic perfume ingredients hastened their demise. But still, each spring, deeply scented purple posies surrounded by their dark green leaves are sold on flower stalls and in florists, albeit on a much smaller scale.

The unscented wild pansy or heartsease, *V. tricolor*, has grown wild in Europe since time out of mind. In Shakespeare's *A Midsummer Night's Dream* its juice, squeezed into Titania's eye, causes her to fall in love with the ass-headed Bottom on awakening. The French knew the flowers as *pensées* or thoughts, which became anglicised to pansies.

The garden pansy that we all grow today arrived in the early nineteenth century. At this time Lady Mary Bennett had pansies in her garden at Walton-on-Thames near London that she planted in a heart-shaped bed. A leading nurseryman of the time, James Lee, worked with her gardener to develop about 20 varieties. Almost simultaneously the gardener to Lord Gambier in Buckinghamshire spotted a rogue seedling with a dark eye. These two novelties heralded the explosion of garden pansies that were swiftly adopted by flower societies, and bred and exhibited throughout the land.

Pansies are grouped as *V. x wittrockiana*. Violas and violettas are complex hybrids of both pansies and violas. *V. cornuta*, the horned violet from the Pyrenees, has given rise to an almost unbelievable choice of varieties, from all colours of the spectrum.

No garden is complete without these long-flowering gems, for they provide excellent edging, thrive in pots and make elegant posies. I love them best in the palest blues, mixed with silver foliage and, underpinning soft pink roses, all combining to create a gentle mist of delicate colours, and the headiest of perfumes.

FLOWERING SEASON: They grow in winter, spring and summer.
SOIL CONDITIONS: Rich soil that drains freely.
SITUATE: In full sunshine.
PROPAGATION: Sow seed under glass in spring, or scatter in the garden at the same time.
RESILIENCE: Mostly they are hardy, but some are frost-prone.
CARE: Keep picking them and they will flower and flower.

OPPOSITE: The charmingly open faces of *V. x wittrockiana* cultivars.

southern bugle lilies

Watsonias flourish in great clumps, looking wonderful against a backdrop of blue sky. Delicate of habit, each perfectly formed flower contributes to the whole, and their colours appear almost iridescent in bright sunshine.

Watsonias were named after a Dr Watson, who was an English apothecary. They grow on the grassy sides of mountains in South Africa and also Madagascar.

Few of the species are scented, which is common in many plants found in South Africa; they are brightly coloured and tend to rely on birds for pollination rather than insects.

Watsonias are not very hardy, but can be planted out once the risk of frosts has passed. *Watsonia marginata* from the Western Cape is a tall clump-forming variety with beautiful flowers of a pale mauve, which have a pleasing perfume. *W. borbonica* has lovely pink flowers, while its sub-species *ardernei* has very delicate white flowers. In the plant-lovers' paradise of Madeira *W. borbonica* ssp. *ardernei* has become naturalised and grows in white drifts along the impressive cliff tops.

It is best to grow watsonia where they are content. They make a demure addition to a border, the upright lance-like foliage enclosing softly coloured spears of flowers with a feathery quality that can help to soften harsher colours.

FLOWERING SEASON: They flower from the onset of spring into summer.
SOIL CONDITIONS: Rich soil that drains freely.
SITUATE: In full sunshine, though they will tolerate some shade.
PROPAGATION: Seed should be sown in autumn. Established clumps can be divided in spring.
RESILIENCE: They are easily damaged by frost.
CARE: Lift the corms in areas that have frost in autumn or, in mild areas, overwinter under a thick mulch.

RIGHT: *Watsonia pyramidata* bears elegant sprays of softly coloured flowers.
OPPOSITE: A clifftop in Madeira is covered with a profusion of *W. borbonica*.

Zantedeschia (Araceae)

calla lily

The pure virginal calla lily is sublime. Imagine a drift of these perfect flowers at dawn, casting an ethereal glow across a landscape or reflected in cool dark still water.

The genus of about six species comes from the east and the south of Africa. They are closely related to the arum lily and in their native habitat grow abundantly in moist areas and at the edges of lakes and streams. Strangely, they are treated with disdain in their homeland, where they are seen as weeds and have the misfortune to be known as pig lilies. There is a tale of a wealthy South African businessman who ordered flowers for his daughter's wedding from a top London florist. On their arrival the bouquets were found to consist of the despised pig lilies. Ever popular at European weddings, they met with derision in their homeland, such are the vagaries of fashion.

Zantedeschia aethiopica, which flowers in summer, is so common in South Africa that it grows prolifically in every suitable spot. The great drifts of its white spathes look incredible to anyone unused to seeing it in profusion. A glorious sight in a rainforest garden in northern Queensland in Australia was of *Z. aethiopica* 'Green Goddess' growing in great bursts and lighting the soft green gloom – the great white spathes edged with purest green looking as if someone had strewn handkerchiefs around.

Z. elliottiana is known as the golden arum. It is a hardy variety that will grow in cooler climates in a sheltered situation. I have some growing in pots in my London garden, where their golden trumpets and white-speckled green foliage are a joy. They survive the winter, but have a perplexing habit of burying their heads in the nearest foliage once in flower.

Hybridised zantedeschias grown for the cut-flower trade come in the most wonderful exotic colours: pinks, yellows, oranges, reds and the deepest purples. The flowers in these photographs lasted for weeks and were greatly admired – altogether a better proposition than their shy golden relatives lurking in the garden.

FLOWERING SEASON: Spring or summer.
SOIL CONDITIONS: Humus rich moist soil.
SITUATE: In full sun.
PROPAGATION: Sow seed when ripe. Dividing in spring.
RESILIENCE: Fully-hardy to frost-tender.
CARE: Protect with deep mulch in frost-prone areas.

RIGHT: The sculptural blooms of the calla lily make it a superb cut flower.
OVERLEAF: The stunning white flowers of *Zantedeschia aethiopica*.

index

A big thank you to all the following for allowing us
to photograph their beautiful gardens…

Ann & Peter Snow, Dunraven, Woomargama, N.S.W
Barry Emerson Irises, Leiston, Suffolk
Belsay Hall, Northumberland
Castle Howard, York, North Yorkshire
Claire Austin, Peonies, Wolverhampton
David Austin, Roses, Wolverhampton
Fairchild Botanical Gardens, Coral Gables, Florida,
   USA
Henry Doubleday Gardens, Kent
Jan & Rod Waddington Nursery, Kiewa valley, N.S.W,
   Australia
Jersey Lavender, Jersey, Channel Islands
John & Helen Richardson, Bellenden Ker,
   Queensland, Australia
John & Lesley Jenkins, Wollerton Old Hall,
   Shropshire
John & Susan Maskelyne, Maulton Nr Newmarket
John Vanderplank, Kingston Seymour Avon U.K.
Kate Campbell, Eye Abbey, Suffolk
Kelways, Langport, Somerset
Les & Elain Musgrove, Fern Brook, Kurrajong
   Heights, N.S.W, Australia
Marylyn Abbott of West Green, Hampshire, UK and
   Kennerton Green Mittagong, N.S.W, Australia
Maureen Thompson Long Melford, Suffolk, UK
Michael & Sarah More-Molyneux, Loseley Park,
   Guildford
Michael & Sophie Hughes, Kingstone Cottage Plants
Mickey Carmichael, Orchids, Fort Lauderdale, Florida
Mr & Mrs Winch of Kettle Hill, Blakeney Norfolk,
   UK
Paul & Jackie Gardner Marston Exotics Medley,
   Hereford, UK
RF Orchids, Homestead Florida
Robert Carvallo, Chateau Villandry, Loire, France
Roger and Wai Davidsons Nurseries. Dural N.S.W
The Wave Botanical Gardens, New York, USA

And to…

The Library at Kew Botanical Gardens
Marco at Angel Flowers, Islington
Rachel Bylykbashi, Sydney, Australia
The Greek Tourist Board and Olympic Airways
Carol Brush, Martha's Vineyard, USA

Bibliography

Austin, David *Old Roses and English Roses*,
   Antique Collectors Club, 1992
Baumann, Helmutt *Greek Wild Flowers & Plant lore
   in Ancient Greece*, Verlag München GMBH (1982)
Bickell, Christopher & Sharman, Fay *The Vanishing
   Garden*, John Murray (1986)
Brickely, Christopher (edited by) *R.H.S A-Z
   Encyclopedia of Garden Plants*
   Dorling Kindersley, (1996)
Coats, Alice *Flowers & their Histories*,
   Hulton Press (1986)
Cobb, James L.S, *Meconopsis*, published in
   association with Hardy Plant Society,
   Christopher Helm Publishers 1989
Genders, Roy *The Scented Flora of the World* ,
   Robert Hale, Ltd. (1997)
Gerard, John *The Herbal* or *General History of
   Plants* (Facsimile edition) 1663 Dover Publications,
   Inc New York, 1975
Grigson, Geoffrey, *The Englishman's Flora*,
   Helicon (1996)
Harvey John, *Medieval Gardens* B.T Batsford (1981)
Huxley & Taylor , *Flowers of Greece and The
   Agean*, Chatto & Windus (1977)
Iatridids, Yanoukos *Flowers of Crete*,
   Published by the author (1985)
Lewis, Peter & Lynch, Margaret, *Campanulas*,
   Christopher Helm (1989)
Meségué, Maurice *Health Secrets of Plants and
   Herbs*, Pan Books In association with William
   Collins & Son (1981)
Parkinson John, *Paradise in Sole Paradisus
   Terrestris* (1629), facsimile, Dover (1976)
Patterson, Allen *Herbs in the Garden*,
   JM Dent & Son (1985)
Robinson, William, *The English Flower Garden*,
   John Murray (1883)
Sanecki, Kay. N *History of the English Herb Garden*,
   Ward Lock, 1992
Step, Edward *Wild Flowers Month by Month in their
   Natural Environment*, FLS, Frederick Warne & Co,
   London & New York, 1906
Stuart, David & Sutherland, James, *Plants from the
   Past* Viking, (1987)
Vickery, Roy, *Oxford Dictionary of Plant work*,
   Oxford University Press (1995)
Wells, Diana *100 flowers & how they got their
   names*, Algonquin Books of Chapel Hill, (1997)
White, Katherine. S, *Onward & Upward in the
   Garden* McGraw & Hill Ryerson, Toronto, (1979)

First published in Canada in 2000 by
New Millennium Books
8036 Enterprise Street
Burnaby, BC, V5A 1V7

Tel: (604) 415-2444; Fax: (604) 415-3444

First published 2000 by Kyle Cathie Limited

ISBN 1-894067-28-2

Text © 2000 Maggie Perry
Photography © 2000 Clay Perry

Designer: Geoff Hayes
Editor: Helen Woodhall
Editorial Assistant: Georgina Burns
Copy-Editor: Sharon Amos
Production: Lorraine Baird and Sha Huxtable

Maggie Perry is hereby identified as the author of this
work in accordance with Section 77 of the Copyright,
Designs and Patents Act 1988.

A Cataloguing In Publication record for this title is
available from the British Library.

Colour separations by Colourscan, Singapore
Printed and bound in Singapore by Tien Wah Press

Thanks to…Sophie Bessemer for all her help during
the teething troubles, to Helen Woodhall, our editor,
for her commitment and energy and Geoff Hayes for
his wonderful design

www.clayperry.com